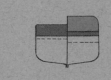

Vessel having top-gallant forecastle with long raised quarter deck & bridge house combined, also known as a well-decked vessel.

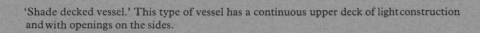

'Shade decked vessel.' This type of vessel has a continuous upper deck of light construction and with openings on the sides.

'Awning decked vessel.' This type of vessel has a continuous upper deck of light construction and sides completely enclosed above the main deck.

'Spar decked vessel.' This type of vessel is constructed with the scantlings above the main deck heavier than in an 'Awning decked vessel' but not so heavy as in a 'three decked vessel'.

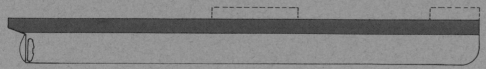

Turret deck vessel.

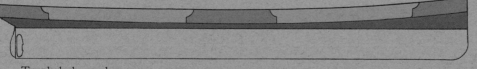

Trunk deck vessel.

(front cover) *Atlas 1* was a derrick pontoon fitted as a coal discharging device on the River Thames in Bugsby's Reach, off Charlton, River Thames. She was owned by a pioneer of the London coal trade, William Cory. (see pp 45–6) (From a painting by Corny Wagner in the National Maritime Museum.)

(back cover) *Clytie* of Whitehaven was a typical steel screw coaster of her day. Built in 1893 by the Ailsa Shipbu[ilding] Co of Troon, she was owned by Robert Simpson of Whitehaven, a[nd] measured 471 tons gross. (From a painting in the National Maritime Museum)

I wish to express my thanks to Mrs E.Tucker, D.J.Lyon and Denis Stonham of the National Maritime Museum, the late D.Ridley Chesterton and the World Ship Society, Michael Jones, Grahame E.Farr, Aled Eames and William Lucas for their valuable help.

Tyne & Wear County Council Museums, 2; Bristol Museum (York Collection), 6, 30, 41, 44; Wisbech & [En]gl[a]nd M[useum], 8 [(top); Royal]

First published 1980

ISBN 0 11 290315 0

Designed by HMSO Graphic Des[ign]

Printed in England for Her Majesty's Stationery Office by W. S. Cowell Ltd, Ipswich

Dd 596284   K160

AD FINEM FIDELIS

Hurl

National Maritime Museum

THE SHIP

Steam Tramps and Cargo Liners
1850–1950

Robin Craig

London
Her Majesty's Stationery Office

Contents

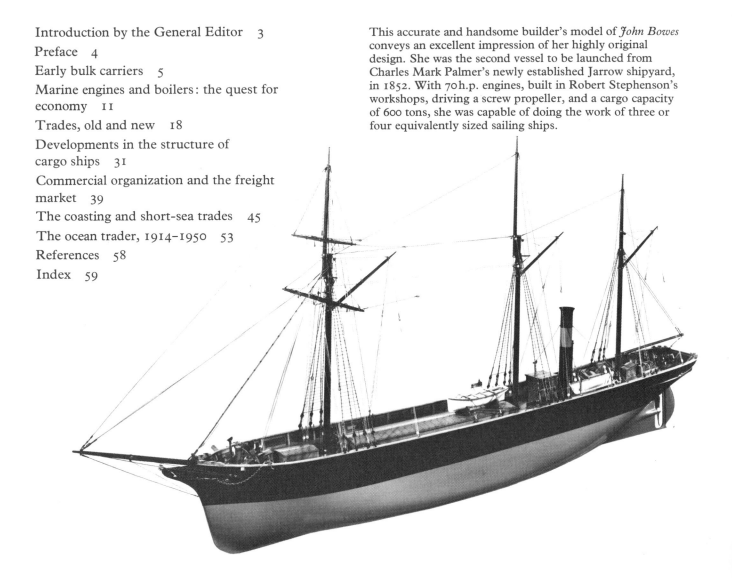

This accurate and handsome builder's model of *John Bowes* conveys an excellent impression of her highly original design. She was the second vessel to be launched from Charles Mark Palmer's newly established Jarrow shipyard, in 1852. With 70 h.p. engines, built in Robert Stephenson's workshops, driving a screw propeller, and a cargo capacity of 600 tons, she was capable of doing the work of three or four equivalently sized sailing ships.

Introduction by the General Editor

This is the fifth of a series of ten short books on the development of the ship, both the merchant vessel and the specialized vessel of war, from the earliest times to the present day, commissioned and produced jointly by the National Maritime Museum and Her Majesty's Stationery Office.

The books are each self-contained, each dealing with one aspect of the subject, but together they cover the evolution of vessels in terms which are detailed, accurate and up-to-date. They incorporate the latest available information and the latest thinking on the subject, but they are readily intelligible to the non-specialist, professional historian or layman.

Above all, as should be expected from the only large and comprehensive general historical museum in the world which deals especially with the impact of the sea on the development of human culture and civilization, the approach is unromantic and realistic. Merchant ships were and are machines for carrying cargo profitably. They carried the trade and, in the words of the very distinguished author of the second book of the series, 'The creation of wealth through trade is at the root of political and military power'. The vessel of war, the maritime vehicle of that power, follows, and she is a machine for men to fight from or with.

It follows from such an approach that the illustrations to this series are for the most part from contemporary sources. The reader can form his own conclusions from the evidence, written and visual. We have not commissioned hypothetical reconstructions, the annotation of which, done properly, would take up much of the text.

The subject of this book is one of the most important in this series. The development of the cargo steamship in the second half of the 19th and the first half of the 20th centuries has been almost completely neglected by maritime, economic and industrial historians. Yet this development played a large part in establishing Britain's economic and political ascendancy at this period and few aspects of our maritime history are as worthy of study.

This neglect has led to widespread false assessment of the relative roles of the steamship and the sailing vessel during this period and to the placing of undue emphasis on the significance in history of single trade operations such as the tea trade from China in clippers which were small in comparison with the total of contemporary merchant shipping activity. The carrying of passengers on schedule liner routes, so ably dealt with by Commander Maber in the next volume in this series, has been studied in a number of books published in the last hundred years, but the spectacular development in the efficiency of the ordinary bulk carrying steamship, which in part made possible the vast industrial expansion of the 40 years before the First World War, although fundamental to the understanding of the history of the period has been almost ignored.

In this little book Robin Craig takes a long step towards remedying this situation. Despite what has so often been said, the 19th century did not see a 'long battle' between sail and steam. For the first 50 years of her life (taking the year of the Battle of Waterloo as a convenient date of effective birth) the steamship presented no real competition to the

Preface

sailing vessel. She provided entirely new services on short-range high density passenger routes, she assisted the sailing vessel as a tug, and as a heavily subsidized mail and passenger carrier on the Atlantic and eastern routes she provided a service which did not exist before. But she could not compete with the mass of sailing vessels which carried the growing trade of the world until the development of the compound engine in the middle 1860's. Thereafter she did successfully penetrate many trades, but a position of relative stability was reached in the 1870's between the bulk carrying steamship and the sailing vessel, which developed rapidly and was now larger and increasingly built of iron. This balance was ended by the introduction of the triple expansion marine steam engine in the 1880's. Then at last the steamship came of age and could operate so economically that she could compete with the big sailing vessel almost anywhere. If there ever was a 'battle' between sail and steam it was a short one in the late 1880's and early 1890's and the result was foreseeable from the start.

Robin Craig spent years in the merchant shipping industry before he took his degree in economic history and became a lecturer at University College London. He is the leading authority in Britain on the development of merchant shipping during the period covered by this book.

Basil Greenhill
DIRECTOR, NATIONAL MARITIME MUSEUM
General Editor

The advent of the cargo-carrying steamship in the 19th century was one of the most important developments in industrial history yet it is almost completely neglected by historians. Writers habitually focus their attention on large passenger liners, implying that they constituted the greatest proportion of the merchant marine. Concentration upon the 'largest', or the 'fastest' gives the wrong impression of what most ships were like, how they had developed, and the purposes for which they were designed.

In this book an attempt is made to describe the influences which promoted the advent of the efficient bulk-carrying steamship, an achievement which is owed to the unique combination of skills displayed by British naval architects and marine engineers, and the vision and risk-taking propensity of several generations of shipowners who ventured their capital in this highly competitive industry. Indeed, it could be argued that the intensity of the competition in cargo-ship construction and operation was the spur to the very high level of functional efficiency which had been attained by such tonnage well before the end of the 19th century.

Early bulk carriers

The decade of the 1840's was remarkable for experiment and innovation, during which the practical cargo-carrying steamship progressed by a tortuous process of trial and error. London's prodigious demand for coal was the principal spur to the new developments, and the main source of supply, the North-East coast of England, furnished many of the new designs. Once the screw propeller and the iron hull had conjoined to manifest their superiority over wooden hulls and paddles, a new impetus was generated by entrepreneurs, shipbuilders and marine engineers who vied with one another in devising novel and enterprising solutions to the intractable problems posed by substituting steam for the large fleet of sailing colliers deployed on the coast between the Tyne and the Thames. As early as 1844 a joint-stock company was registered with a capital of £500000 to 'carry coals to London and elsewhere by steam'. This firm, the General Steam Collier Company, proved abortive, but its intentions were a straw in the wind.

Earlier, in 1842, the iron twin screw *Bedlington*, 277 tons gross, was built by that highly innovative shipbuilder, Thomas Dunn Marshall of South Shields, intended to convey coal from Blyth to South Shields. She embodied several new features, including a double bottom for the carriage of water-ballast, and revolutionary methods of loading and discharge. Lloyd's Survey report, dated 22 September 1842, described her as follows:

This vessel is fitted on the floors with rails for waggons to be run fore and aft and calculated to contain 40 waggons, fitted with a working drop to answer either side over the main hatchway which is adapted to hoist and lower by the engine that drives the propelling screws which are fitted in each run. The boilers are placed closed [sic] forward and the engines aft, leaving the entire hold amidships for the stowage of the waggons on the four railways.[1]

Rarely can a sea-going vessel have embraced so many novel features, anticipating by several generations the rail ferry and the roll-on-roll-off ship. She cost her owners, the Bedlington Coal Company, £4925. *Bedlington* was soon followed by the iron auxiliary screw steamer *QED* of 1844, built by John Coutts of Walker, and engined by Messrs. Hawthorn with 20 h.p. engines driving 'Mr Smiths patent screw'.[2] She was also fitted with four bulkheads and a double bottom for water-ballast. She was designed to carry 340 tons of coal. *Experiment*, a 409-ton gross screw steamer built by Thomas Rountree at Sunderland in the following year reverted to wood construction, and was lost by fire soon after being commissioned, whilst T.D.Marshall launched *Conside* expressly for the London trade in 1847: she measured 387 tons gross. Clyde shipbuilders, not to be outdone, responded in 1848 with the iron screw *Collier* built by John Reid at Port Glasgow. Of 157 tons gross, engined by Caird and Company at Greenock, this vessel enjoyed a long and varied career which included a deep-sea voyage to Australia in 1854. She survived until the eve of the First World War. In this respect, *Collier* differed materially from her predecessors, since the earlier experimental vessels had very short lives, suffering from defects of design or chance maritime disaster.

The iron screw steamer *Collier* was built by John Reid at Port Glasgow in 1848 and was one of the earliest, albeit one of the smallest, bulk cargo carriers. Originally she was 157 tons gross, but she was lengthened by nearly 33 feet in 1857 which increased her tonnage to 195. Her 40 h.p. engines were built by Caird & Co of Greenock, and gave her a top speed of 10 knots, but her average speed was about 7 knots at which speed she burned about 4½ tons of coal a day. Originally fitted with wooden bulwarks and three masts, this little steamship was much altered in the course of a long life. This photograph was probably taken in the year 1908, as she neared her end.

The most successful of these pioneer steam screw colliers was unquestionably *John Bowes*, built by Charles Mark Palmer at his Jarrow Shipyard in 1852, at a cost of £10000. On a gross tonnage of 486, she measured 148.9 feet in length, 25.7 in breadth and 15.6 feet in depth and had a cargo capacity of 600 tons. She was given 60 h.p. engines by Robert Stephenson of Newcastle. This notable vessel established the iron screw collier as a commercially profitable investment, but it was many years before such vessels assumed an unchallengeable advantage over sailing vessels in the coal trade. As late as 1863, three-quarters of seaborne coal to London was carried by sail and only one-quarter by steamer. But Palmer built 25 vessels embodying the main concepts incorporated in *John Bowes* within two years of her launch, and the future of such vessels was assured, despite many subsequent setbacks and disappointments. Her builder, speaking in 1863, recalled that on her first trip to London she was laden with 650 tons of coal in four hours; in 48 hours she arrived in London; in 24 hours she discharged her cargo; and in 48 hours more she was again in the River Tyne.[3] In five days she performed successfully an amount of work that would have taken two average-sized sailing colliers upwards of a month to accomplish. Palmer went on to point out that, in 1852, screw colliers made 17 voyages to London laden with an aggregate 9483 tons of cargo: in 1862, 1472 cargoes were carried by screw collier, totalling nearly one million tons. *John Bowes* had a long life: she was given new engines in 1864, and again in 1883, and was also reboiled more than once. She was sold to Norwegian owners in 1898 for £1500; and purchased by Spaniards in 1908 for £2000, who kept her at work until she was finally lost by foundering in 1933.

The design of the early iron screw steamers posed problems that were not easily solved. As notable a naval architect as John Scott Russell thought that such cargo ships posed the most intractable problems of all for designers. These vessels had of necessity to be economical in the use of fuel in order that the revenue-earning space (that is, cargo capacity) be maximized, and voyage costs kept low by econo-mizing on bunker space, stokers and firemen. Until marine engines became relatively efficient, after the advent of the compound engine, the problem of fuel consumption remained a challenging one, and screw steamers were limited to voyages of only a few days' steaming without rebunkering. Thus, until the early 1860's voyages were mainly confined to the coasts of Great Britain and Ireland, the near Continental ports, and the Baltic, where refuelling expenses and the price of coal alike were low. More distant voyages required more fuel and thus a better economic return was necessary. This was best achieved by the carriage of high value, low volume cargo carried on a liner basis, and entrepreneurs who established these services were able to extend trade considerably, especially to the Mediterranean where it was possible to establish convenient bunkering stations.

One of the problems encountered with bulk-carrying screw steamers was the need for these vessels to be properly ballasted and trimmed, especially when no cargo was being carried – and most steam colliers had to make a high proportion of ballast trips. Sailing vessels and the pioneer screw steam vessels had to carry solid ballast in order to maintain stability and trim in all conditions at sea, and the loading and discharge of materials such as stone, chalk or gravel was an expense in time and money which the steamship owner could ill afford. Furthermore, dock and harbour authorities were always extremely concerned about the promiscuous discharge of ballast. This could play havoc with waterways and channels which had to be dredged at great expense to maintain or increase the depth of water that the new types of ship required for their employment.

Among the experimental ballasting devices at first adopted was a system of collapsible canvas bags which could be filled with water on ballast voyages. *John Bowes* was at first fitted with these, but the system was soon abandoned as impracticable since the canvas was so easily damaged or punctured. The design of iron ships with tanks to carry water-ballast was the obvious solution, since water could be pumped in and out quite independently of the vessel's cargo work, using power from the ships engines. A centre water-ballast tank was advocated by, among others, John Scott Russell, and formed one of the illustrations to his great treatise on naval architecture,[4] but this system imposed great strains on the hull, and detracted considerably from the cargo-carrying potential of the vessel. John McIntyre, of Palmer's shipyard, introduced the most wide-spread method of accommodating water-ballast, and the 'McIntyre tank' was widely adopted after its first use in the iron screw steamer *Samuel Laing*, built in 1854. McIntyre's system required the construction of permanent water-ballast tanks laid on top of the floor plates of the ship strengthened by a series of longitudinals. On top of these an inner bottom was fitted so that, in effect, the vessel had a double bottom in which to carry water-ballast which could be loaded or emptied very quickly to ensure optimal trim. The exigencies of new trades, especially heavy or bulky cargoes, called forth alternative systems of ballasting in the 1870's and 1880's: for example, the cellular double bottom was introduced in the iron screw steamer *Fenton*, built in 1876 by Hunter & Austin of Sunderland. Of 784 tons gross, with a

length of 200.8 feet, her cellular double bottom extended 126 feet. Other developments included the introduction of fore and aft peak tanks and wing and side tanks: wing tanks were widely adopted for specialized cargo such as iron ore in the 1880's.

Three other problems arose in connexion with the advent of the iron ship, and deserve passing reference. First, compasses were adversely affected by the introduction of iron construction and several important maritime disasters were attributed to the failure to recognize the need to adjust compasses for error. Secondly, iron ship construction posed great

This photograph was taken by the celebrated photographer Samuel Smith at Wisbech on 8 August 1853. It portrays the iron screw collier *Lady Alice Lambton* newly built by T.D.Marshall at South Shields for Richard Young, a Wisbech coal merchant and shipowner, whose new house was being built at the time and is seen in the background. This typical collier was fitted with waterproof bags for the carriage of water-ballast – a method soon to be superseded by the installation of the permanent 'McIntyre tank'. Capable of carrying 700 tons of coal, *Lady Alice Lambton* was soon to be employed as a transport during the Crimean War, and was lost by collision in 1862.

'She combines at the same time the character of a sailing ship, a steamer and also a passenger steamer' wrote Alexander Stephen of Kelvinhaugh, River Clyde, her builder, to Henry Bath of Swansea, her owner. *Zeta* was one of the few auxiliary screw steamers designed to carry a bulk cargo in a deep-sea trade, being intended for the copper ore trade between Chile and Swansea in 1865, a route upon which sailing ships predominated because of the absence of convenient bunkering stations for steamships. *Zeta*'s engines were designed by J.F.Spencer, Bath's son-in-law and designer of Stephen's Linthouse shipyard, who founded a famous marine engineering enterprise in Sunderland.

problems of marine fouling which had a highly deleterious effect upon the effective efficiency of steamships at sea until the problem had been counteracted by the introduction of anti-fouling paints and compositions. These had achieved a very fair measure of success by the early 1870's. Finally, iron hulls at first proved unpopular with many shippers because sweating and taint damaged many cargoes. This was an important cause of complaint among, for example, the shippers of tea from China after the introduction of iron steamers in the trade before the opening of the Suez Canal. Naval architects had to learn to make proper arrangements for the efficient ventilation of cargo space so that the prejudice against shipping valuable freights in iron vessels could be dissipated.

When Samuel Seaward addressed the Institute of Civil Engineers in 1842[5] he supposed that the existing boundary of steam voyages was 20 days' steaming. He and many of his contemporaries advocated a compromise solution to the problem of sustaining commercially profitable steam communication over long distances by utilizing a combination of screw propulsion and sails. The auxiliary steamer would, it was thought, serve to extend the possible limits of the steamship in the more distant trades by making use of wind whenever favourable but by installing relatively small engines to drive a propeller which could be lifted when required, sufficient fuel economy could be achieved to permit the carriage of a profitable pay load of freight. These ideas persisted thanks to the advocacy of Seaward and, for example, W.S.Lindsay, who in later years was to write a formidable *History of Merchant Shipping*.

Lindsay, among others, invested heavily in auxiliary steamers with a view to conquering for steam some of the long-distance trades, such as that to Australia. But, as one recent writer has expressed it 'On no important trade route in the world were steamships in the 1860's so ineffectual in capturing traffic from pure sailing ships'.[6] Passengers on some of the auxiliary steamers would have readily agreed. Lindsay's houseflag, which proudly displayed the initials W.S.L., was thought by one humourist to be an abbreviation of 'Worst Steamship Line'. Auxiliary steamers were soon superseded on nearly all routes by the compound-engined vessel which was to have a revolutionary effect upon the rôle of the steamship in oceanic trade. Before we turn to the compound engine, however, we must note one other vessel that was designed to embody the advantages of both sail and steam. She was the iron barque-rigged auxiliary screw steamer *Zeta*, designed by J.F.Spencer and built by Alexander Stephen at his Kelvinhaugh shipyard for the Swansea firm of H.Bath & Company in 1865. *Zeta* was built for specialized, very demanding employment, the copper ore trade between the West Coast of South America and Swansea. Cargoes of copper ore required great skill and care in stowage and vessels were fitted with a 'trunk' to raise the cargo in the hold so that the centre of gravity would not be too low, causing the ship to be excessively stiff at sea. But it was not just the cargo that posed problems: it was the fact that ships in the trade were required to 'double' the notorious Cape Horn: that is, they had to sail both from west to east and from east to west round the southernmost Cape of South America very often in extreme weather. The particular reason for adopting auxiliary engines on this route, however, was not merely dictated by the cargoes to be carried or the weather to be encountered, but by the complete absence of conveniently placed bunkering stations that would permit conventional steamers to refuel. *Zeta*, like other auxiliary steamers, was a brave compromise: however, she was not a commercial success, and the sailing vessel survived in the Cape Horn trade for at least another 45 years.

Marine engines and boilers: the quest for economy

Little could be done to extend the range and economy of the steamship until some means had been found whereby the consumption of coal could be effectively reduced. Fuel economy was achieved when the compound principle, already adopted in land steam engines and in a few small experimental steamboats, was applied to the sea-going ship by the Scottish engineers John Elder and Charles Randolph who designed and built the first ocean-going compound engines for the steamship *Brandon* (764 tons gross), in 1854. This firm, Randolph, Elder & Co, had already built similar engines for factory use. On her trial trip in July 1854, *Brandon's* consumption of coal was about $3\frac{1}{4}$ lbs per IHP per hour, compared with her most economical predecessor's consumption of 4 or $4\frac{1}{2}$ lbs per IHP. The economy of fuel demonstrated by this vessel (of the order of 30 or 40 per cent) was not lost on other ship owners whose fuel costs were exceptionally high.

The Pacific Steam Navigation Company soon selected compound engines for their paddle steamers *Valparaiso* and *Inca*, built in 1856, as their vessels plied on the west coast of South America where coals were very expensive and bunkering stations few and far between. For similar reasons, Peninsular &

The introduction of the triple expansion engine gave a tremendous impetus to the commercial application of the steamship. This 1:12 scale model of such an engine was made by E.B.Wilcox of Weaverham, Cheshire, and presented to Liverpool Public Museums. The model is of an engine of about 350 indicated horse-power, which would be sufficient to power a typical short-sea trader in the late 19th century.

Oriental, whose vessels were regularly committed to the extended route to the Far East, followed suit, and *Mooltan*, delivered in 1861, was to be the first of many P&O vessels equipped with compound engines. But it would be misleading to suppose that the compound engine was a complete success from the outset. The economy of fuel could not be gainsaid, but the development of compound engines was undoubtedly delayed by the poor quality of boilers. Despite the purchase of carefully selected fuel, and the employment of specially trained engineers, it was found, in many early P&O compound-engined vessels, that it was impossible to sustain proper working pressure because of poor boiler design. One observer graphically described the experience of sailing in P&O vessels at this time:

Piston rods and valve spindles as black as coal tar; slide valves chirping like a cageful of canaries; low-pressure pistons thumping like big drums, softened occasionally by water through the indicator cocks, to prevent the whole fabric coming down.[7]

He went on to relate that the strain occasioned to the engineers on board these vessels was sometimes so great that four of them might well be ill at the same time during the trying passage through the Red Sea.

The early compound engines were worked at a steam pressure of no more than 30 psi, and before the 1860's Randolph, Elder & Co used the ordinary jet condenser. Thereafter, the surface condenser was introduced, and higher pressures of steam were applied: 40 lbs in the early 1860's, 60 lbs by 1866 and 70 lbs by the mid-1870's. These progressive

improvements owed not a little to better boilers, and improved boiler design depended critically upon better quality mild steel.

Some of the success of the compound engine in the working of cargo steamers is attributed to the enterprise and skill of Alfred Holt, who, significantly, was trained as an engineer before he became a shipowner and founder of the celebrated Blue Funnel Line.[8] Alfred Holt first experimented with his own design of tandem compound engine in the iron screw steamer *Cleator*, built for the iron ore and coal trade of Cumberland, the former mainly shipped to South Wales. *Cleator* was re-engined to Holt's specification in 1864, with her boiler pressure raised to 60 psi.

Agamemnon was built by Scott & Co, Greenock in 1866 to the order of Alfred Holt of Liverpool, founder of the famous Blue Funnel Line. She was the pioneer steamship in Holt's fleet and fitted with the compound tandem engines which he had designed. On her trials, the vessel consumed no more than $20\frac{1}{4}$ tons of coal in 24 hours and Holt wrote 'this result as far as I know is not approached by any vessel afloat'. *Agamemnon* could carry 3500 tons of cargo and was deployed on the route to China via Cape of Good Hope, competing successfully with the celebrated 'tea clippers' that had dominated the tea trade. She cost £52 000.

'The Managers have ordered four more steamers, larger and faster than any previously possessed', wrote Alfred Holt & Co of their 1895–6 building programme. *Prometheus* was built by Scott & Co, Greenock, at a cost of £62 558. She registered 5570 tons gross and had triple expansion engines of 590 nominal horse-power.

Peleus was one of the 'P' class cargo and passenger liners built by Cammell, Laird & Co Ltd, Birkenhead, for Alfred Holt's Ocean Steam Ship Company in 1949. Of 10 093 tons gross, she carried 11 270 tons deadweight besides 30 passengers, and was fitted for refrigerated cargo. Her three steam turbines were double-reduction geared to her screw shaft to give a service speed of 18 knots. Comparison with *Agamemnon* (1866) and *Prometheus* (1896) graphically illustrates over 70 years of progress in the design of first-class cargo ships.

The new engines proved dramatically successful: the ship was not only faster, but consumed almost 40 per cent less fuel, which meant that she was able to extend the range of her voyages from the coastwise trade for which she had originally been designed, to as far afield as Brazil – a trip impossible with her old engines unless most of her cargo space had been devoted to the carriage of coal necessary for her to complete her passage.

Holt's enterprise was thus justified, and he embarked upon an ambitious plan to inaugurate a steamship service to the Far East via the Cape of Good Hope, the success of which depended critically upon the compound engine. Scott of Greenock received a £156 000 order to build three large iron screw steamers which embodied Holt's engine design. The three vessels, *Agamemnon*, *Ajax* and *Achilles*, built in 1865-6, formed the first units in the fleet of the Ocean Steam Ship Company and proved an historic turning point in British maritime history. The opening of the Suez Canal in 1869 confirmed the foresight of Alfred Holt, since it then became possible for him to reduce the length of passage to the East by 10 or 12 days' steaming, thus securing for the firm an increasing share of the profitable Far Eastern trade. The days of the full-rigged sailing clippers engaged in the tea trade from China to Britain were thereafter numbered: by the late 1870's few of these magnificent vessels could compete in the lucrative and well-publicized tea run to London.

Compound engines were widely adopted in the 1860's and 1870's and with this advance in marine propulsion, Britain's superiority in the construction and operation of iron screw steamers was made absolute. The introduction of higher boiler pressures and a higher speed of piston, led to economy in fuel consumption and this was reinforced by lighter engines which took less space in the hulls of the steamships in which they were installed. A commentator pointed out in the mid-1880's that the weight of machinery had a very significant effect on profits: economy of fuel was not enough by itself if it required a sacrifice of space or added weight. He suggested that every ton of deadweight capacity was worth on average £10 a year in freight: so that a 100 tons saving in engine weight could mean £1000 a year additional income to owners.[9]

As cargo capacity was greatly increased, so the number of stokers and firemen required to maintain a given speed at sea was steadily reduced. Other innovations also enhanced the performance of cargo-carrying ships during these decades of rapid technological advance, notably the installation of superheaters, which again permitted notable reductions in fuel consumption, and the more widespread introduction of forced draught, a feature of an American auxiliary steamer as early as 1845 or 1846, but not widely adopted until much later. By the 1880's it was claimed that forced draught could reduce the consumption of coal by as much as 15 per cent, but no less important, it could mean that coal of much poorer quality (therefore costing less) could be utilized in steamships.[10] The significance of this may be demonstrated by the evidence of one writer who pointed out that coal costs represented about 18 per cent of the voyage costs of a 2500 deadweight-ton vessel in 1872.[11]

In 1880 an 1864-built steamer named *Propontis* was fitted with the first triple expansion engines by Alexander Kirk, then manager of John Elder & Co. This innovation demonstrated the benefits to be derived from the expansion of steam in three stages, which further economized in fuel consumption. However, just as confidence in the early compound engines was sometimes shaken, not because of the faults in the concept, but because of the defective boiler design, so *Propontis* proved unreliable because her boilers were unable to sustain the required high pressure steam. Fortunately, the introduction of Siemens steel wrought improvements in boiler design and construction and the triple expansion engine was demonstrated with complete success in the iron screw steamer *Aberdeen*, built in 1881 by R.Napier & Sons for the Australian trade of G.Thompson & Co, of Aberdeen. This vessel, of 3616 tons gross, had cylindrical, double-ended steel boilers working at a pressure of 125 psi, and on her maiden voyage to Melbourne coal consumption was as little as $1\frac{1}{4}$ lbs per IHP per hour.

It was only a matter of two or three years before the manifest economies of the triple expansion engine were so generally apparent that it was widely adopted, especially in the economical cargo liners and tramps which played so large a part in demonstrating the technical superiority of British ship design for another generation. By 1891 it was claimed that fuel economy in cargo steamers was 20 per cent superior to the best practice prevailing 10 years earlier. A comparison of best practice in the years 1872, 1881, 1891, and 1901 may be summarised thus:

	1872	1881	1891	1901 [12]
Boiler pressure, lbs per sq.inch.	52.4	77.4	158.5	197
Revolutions per minute.	55.67	59.76	63.75	87
Piston speed: ft.per min.	376	467	529	654
Coal consumption: per hp per hr, lbs.	2.110	1.828	1.522	1.48

Expressed in economic terms, J.P.Hall pointed out in 1886, that for a 3000 tons deadweight vessel of 9 or $9\frac{1}{2}$ knots, with an average number of 250 steaming days per annum, triple expansion engines would save shipowners investing in them £1000 a year. If such a vessel was reckoned to cost £23000, this would be equal to a dividend of 4.34 per cent per annum.[13] Despite an increase in the cost of coal in real terms of 5/- per ton between 1885 and 1890, actual bunkering costs had not increased during these years, thanks to the marked improvement in the efficiency of marine engines.

By the middle of the 1890's prodigies of economy had been attained in ordinary cargo steamers. *Oscar II*, a trunk-decked vessel built by William Gray & Co of West Hartlepool in 1891, could carry 4600 tons deadweight of cargo on 14 tons of coal per day at 9 knots, this being equal to coal consumption of half an ounce of coal per ton per knot – scarcely more than the energy released by the burning of a couple of sheets of writing paper.[14]

Not every technical achievement, however, justified itself. Some advanced designs failed to live up to expectations because the design of marine engines and boilers could not be considered in isolation from other equally pressing considerations. Some shipbuilders, in seeking to emphasize one desirable quality in the cargo ship, were forced to sacrifice others. This appeared to be the case in the steamers William Gray & Co, of West Hartlepool built for Hamilton, Fraser & Co, beginning with *Inchmona*, 3484 tons gross, 5005 deadweight, built in 1896. This ship had five cylinders and operated at a boiler pressure of 225 psi, and the builders guaranteed the owners a coal consumption of 1.15 lbs per IHP per hour. Although several such vessels were built, they were not an unqualified success since the added length of the engine room to accommodate the five cylinder engines detracted from cargo carrying capacity. In this case there was a diminution of earning power which was not fully compensated for by greater fuel economy.

For similar reasons, the invention of the turbine had comparatively little early impact on conventional cargo ships. The high initial cost of the installation of turbines, and the modest economical speed of the cargo liner/tramp, combined to render the adoption of the steam turbine as inappropriate for this class of vessel. Nevertheless, attempts were made to determine the extent to which the turbine, linked with mechanical gearing between turbine and screw shaft, might be made economically justifiable for conventional cargo ships. To this end, the steamship *Vespasian*, 2147 tons gross, built as *Eastern Prince* in 1887, was purchased and fitted with geared turbines. The success of this experiment seemed to justify the installation of turbines in a newly designed vessel and *Cairnross*, 4016 tons gross, was built by William Doxford & Sons of Sunderland in 1913, her perform-

ance comparing favourably with *Cairngowan*, built two years earlier to an identical hull design, but with conventional triple expansion engines. *Cairnross* proved more economical on comparative trials and her coal consumption was about 15 per cent less than

The steel screw steamer *Cairnross* was the first cargo steamer to be specially designed to be powered by geared turbines, which were manufactured by Parsons Marine Steam Turbine Ltd, of Newcastle. In other respects, she was a conventional cargo steamer of her period. She was launched from William Doxford's Sunderland shipyard in 1913 for Cairn Line of Steamships Ltd, of which Cairns, Noble & Co, of Newcastle were managers. Of 4016 tons gross, she had a deadweight of 7830 tons, and proved more economical in fuel consumption than her conventionally engined sistership *Cairngowan*.

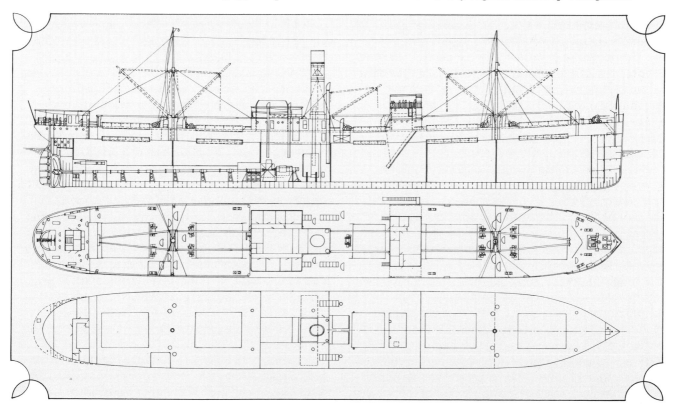

the older vessel. Her machinery weighed about 20 tons less than the reciprocating engines in *Cairngowan*, which should have rendered the turbine steamer a more profitable venture. It was not clear, however, that the higher prime cost of the geared turbines was adequately compensated for by her expected revenue. For faster ships in more specialized trades, however, turbines proved themselves more appropriate. In 1908 Denny's of Dumbarton built *Otaki*, for the New Zealand Shipping Company, the first merchant steamer to have a combination of reciprocating and turbine machinery. With two wing shafts driven by reciprocating engines, her centre shaft was driven by a low-pressure turbine which took its steam from the reciprocating engine's exhaust. This vessel was built expressly for the frozen meat trade, and therefore was designed to sustain a speed in excess of that regarded as economic for the ordinary dry cargo tramp. *Otaki* was designed to carry 9900 tons deadweight (100 000 carcasses of mutton) on a draught of $27\frac{1}{2}$ feet. She was guaranteed by her builders to make 14 knots carrying 5000 tons deadweight. Her price was £123 910 on which her builders sustained a loss of £9880.[15]

The vast generality of cargo ships were content with a slower speed in the interest of economy in coal consumption, which was of the utmost importance to the tramp shipowner. There were other necessary qualities as well, including uncomplicated engine construction, reliability, ease of maintenance, and, not least, simplicity in day-to-day operation. Elaborate, complex marine engines proved exceptionally costly to maintain. The requirement of an endless supply of spare parts could prove expensive in the mundane exigencies of tramp ship operation in which delays were costly. Good engine-room staff were at a premium: every shipowner had to consider very carefully if more experienced personnel might be required to man more complex engine rooms, and

it was not clear that complicated installations were the best means of obtaining a tolerable return on what would almost certainly be a higher prime cost. Even firemen could have a profound effect upon economy at sea: there is plenty of evidence to suggest that competent firemen could enormously enhance the revenue-earning potential of the merchant ship. Conversely, inefficient stokers and firemen could render largely nugatory some more advanced innovation calculated to improve efficiency. Given the character of the labour force available, most shipowners were understandably conservative in their approach to extreme innovation.

This conservatism was made manifest with the introduction of the internal combustion engine as a new type of prime mover for deep-sea ships in the years immediately preceding the First World War. The launch of the celebrated Danish motor vessel *Selandia*, built and engined by Burmeister and Wain of Copenhagen for the East Asiatic Company of Copenhagen, was an event which was to have deep and long-term effects on the world's merchant fleets. With a deadweight of 7400 tons, and accommodation for 24 passengers, *Selandia* had two sets of four-stroke-cycle single-acting diesel engines producing 2500 IHP at about 140 rpm. At this rating her fuel consumption was no more than ten tons per day and since she was able to carry most of her fuel in her double bottom, she was capable of making a round trip from Europe to the Far East and back without replenishing her bunkers. With her sisterships, *Fionia*, also built by Burmeister & Wain, and *Jutlandia*, built by Barclay, Curle & Co, on the Clyde, the three vessels gave substantial impetus to the widespread introduction of diesel marine engines. Significantly, the East Asiatic Company never looked back, henceforth opting for diesel propulsion in all their vessels. However, most shipowners in Britain proved more sceptical, although one or two became enthusiastic supporters of this new and pathbreaking mode of marine propulsion.

One other factor contributed to the increasing efficiency of ships in the years before 1914 and after. This was the simple expedient of substituting the burning of oil fuel for coal. The use of substances such as creosote had been advocated by Captain (later Vice-Admiral) Selwyn in the late 1860's: at that time it was widely thought that it was too risky to burn fuel oil. However, some early tank steamers on the Caspian Sea and on the River Volga were burning *Astatki* (oil refinery residue) in the 1860's, and there were oil-burning steamers on the Caspian from 1870.

Tankers were among the first ships to use oil fuel in the deep-sea trades. Shell Transport and Trading's *Strombus* (built by Armstrong, Whitworth and Company, Newcastle, in 1900, 6030 tons gross) brought a cargo of rice from Saigon to Hamburg in 1902 and then shipped 800 tons of liquid fuel at Thameshaven preparatory to a voyage to USA to load Texas oil for UK. When using Welsh coal *Strombus* consumed 42–43 tons per day, but her oil consumption was only 28 to 30 tons: moreover, using oil fuel, six men were able to do the work of the 26 normally employed in the stokehold.[16]

Despite such striking demonstrations of economy, the high price and imperfect distribution of oil fuel were the main constraints on its use before the First World War, but, in the course of time, oil fuel was destined to achieve widespread use: apart from its obvious commercial advantages, it transformed the lives of those unfortunates who went to sea as stokers, firemen and trimmers.

Selandia, pictured here in the port of London, embodied so many novel features that she might well be regarded as one of the most original ships ever built. Her appearance was strikingly different from other ships of her time. With her 'four island' profile, her three masts, and with the absence of a funnel she was the first large ocean-going vessel to be propelled by diesel engines. Built by Burmeister & Wain of Copenhagen in 1912, she was the first of three similar vessels, one of which was built by Barclay, Curle & Co at Glasgow. Of 4950 tons gross, she carried about 7500 tons of cargo, and enough diesel fuel in her double bottom to cover 30 000 miles at her designed speed of 11 knots. Owned by the East Asiatic Company of Copenhagen, she was employed in their Far Eastern service. After changes of owners and name, she was lost in 1942.

Trades, old and new

The technical changes in cargo steamers were the consequence of a number of powerful economic influences, of which Britain's unprecedented industrial and commercial growth in the 19th century was the most important. This growth was accompanied by a rapid increase in population, and the consequential demand for all kinds of goods and services was further enhanced by emigration and colonialization on a massive scale. New technology was demanded and supplied, and the process in turn required new products, new methods of production, and particularly important in our context, new raw materials and new sources of supply. This widening web of commerce is often measured in value terms, but for shipowners it was volume not value that was the significant variable. One statistician reckoned that there was a sevenfold increase in seaborne commerce between 1840 and 1887. He enumerated the growth as shown in the adjacent table.

These figures disguise rather than reveal the true extent in the expansion of demand for shipping services. Take, for example, just two items, wool and grain. In the 1840's Britain was the biggest market for both, and both commodities were supplied from the Western seaboard of Continental Europe. As new regions were settled and became agriculturally productive, new sources of supply vied with, then replaced, the old. The Baltic region ceased to be the major source of breadstuffs, and Germany no longer supplied much of Britain's requirement of wool. After Corn Law repeal, and with the establishment of Free Trade, Britain was supplied from more distant regions – wool from Australia, and breadstuffs from the Black Sea, the United States and elsewhere. By the 1880's, moreover, it was not just America's eastern seaboard that supplied wheat, but Californian crops formed an important part of Britain's import requirements, involving the long haul round Cape Horn. These new and attenuated trade routes had marked effects upon the growth in the demand for shipping. They meant that proportionately more shipping was required, despite the increase in productivity that the steamship introduced.

New commodities entered into world commerce in the 19th century. Jute was one of these, a commodity that required many ships deployed on a long haul. This traffic was partly a function of the growth of

Merchandise carried by sea, annual totals, 1840 and 1887 ('000 tons)

Commodity	1840	1887	17
Coal	1400	49300	
Iron	1100	11800	
Timber	4100	12100	
Grain	1900	19200	
Sugar	700	4400	
Petroleum	—	2700	
Cotton	400	1800	
Wool	20	350	
Jute	—	600	
Meat	—	700	
Coffee	200	600	
Wine	200	1400	
Salt	800	1300	
Sundries	9180	33750	
Total	20000	140000	

that in grain, since grain and related products needed bagging, especially as ships and cargoes increased in size and regulations were introduced to diminish the risk of cargo shifting – a danger reduced by regulations requiring part of each cargo to be shipped in bags.

But perhaps the most dramatic increase was the trade in metallic ore. The early stages of industrialization in Britain had been met by an almost total dependence upon domestic ore sources, both ferrous and non-ferrous. From the early decades of the 19th century, however, there was to be a remarkable change as domestic ore supplies were worked out. Iron ore, copper ore, zinc ore and pyrites were imported in large quantities, and the shipping industry found itself handling new types of cargo, having particularly difficult characteristics, in unprecedented quantities. The bulk carriage of liquids, particularly hazardous liquids such as petroleum, was also to present shipbuilders with a new challenge, and the advent of the tanker deserves particular consideration, since it illustrates some of the problems with which naval architects, shipbuilders and shipowners had to contend.

The shipment of petroleum began in 1861 when a small consignment of five barrels was shipped across the Atlantic from America. Later in that same year the wooden brig *Elizabeth Watts* of 224 tons loaded a complete cargo of petroleum in barrels from Philadelphia to London, and the Transatlantic trade in petroleum grew rapidly. Two methods of shipping were at first adopted: either the petroleum was shipped in barrels, or in tinplate boxes with an outside covering of wood. Both these methods were costly and wasteful: the barrels and cases themselves were expensive, and much broken stowage was inevitable, with the vessels employed unable to load their full deadweight. Moreover, there was a good deal of leakage – generally two per cent was allowed for, and this in itself was both wasteful and highly dangerous. Explosions were common, as reference to the 1867 edition of R.W.Stevens' *The Stowage of Ships* would reveal.

Not unnaturally, entrepreneurs turned their attention to the possibility of shipping petroleum in bulk, and several designers produced plans from the early 1860's onwards. T.C.Gibson of Ramsey, Isle of Man, applied for a patent in 1862, and a vessel called *Ramsey*, 821 tons, was constructed on the island. Two other vessels were built on the Tyne at about the same time, but these vessels were soon withdrawn from the trade. Palmer Brothers of Jarrow, who had pioneered the screw collier, built in 1872 the first steamer designed to carry petroleum, but *Vaderland*, 2748 tons gross, despite having some of the characteristics of later tanker design – she had engines aft, transverse and longitudinal bulkheads, and expansion tanks – was refused facilities to discharge at Antwerp by the authorities, who would not permit tanks to be constructed to store the cargo. Two later vessels, *Nederland*, built in 1873 and *Switzerland* (1874), were built with engines amidships, but never actually loaded petroleum.

Fergusons of 1885 was a dry cargo ship, built by Bartram and Haswell of Sunderland and converted by Craggs and Sons, and was expressly altered into a tanker for the Russian oil trade which was becoming increasingly important in the 1880's. This vessel was the first to bring a cargo of petroleum from Batoum to the United Kingdom. She was fitted with a system of 32 tanks with four additional regulating tanks: unfortunately, she suffered the fate of many early tankers when, in 1889, she exploded, burnt and sank in the French port of Rouen. Another vessel, the steamship *Chigwell*, was purchased by that pioneer of early tankers, Alfred Suart, and similarly converted for the carriage of petroleum from the Russian oilfields.

Several of the first ocean-going tankers were converted dry cargo ships, of which the iron steamship *Chigwell* was one. Built at Sunderland by Bartram, Haswell & Co in 1883, she is seen here at Gravesend in the 1890s, and was owned by that pioneer tanker owner A.Suart of London.

Despite some criticism that British ship designers were slow to solve the difficult problems of carrying petroleum in bulk in specially designed vessels, it is noteworthy that Henry F. Swan took out a patent which was embodied in the first real oil tanker to be constructed, *Gluckhauf*, completed in 1886 by the shipbuilders Sir W.G.Armstrong, Mitchell and Co. Of 2307 tons gross, with a speed of 11 knots, she discharged her first cargo at Geestemunde in July 1886, having been built to the order of Heinrich Riedemann of Bremen, who had previously experimented with iron sailing vessels for this new trade. The advantages procured by constructing specialized iron screw tankers were soon made manifest, despite the hazardous nature of the cargo: an older type vessel equivalent in size to *Gluckhauf* might ship 12120 barrels requiring three or four weeks to load, whereas *Gluckhauf* took three days or less to take in her cargo and could carry the equivalent of 23000 barrels. One commentator suggested that a shipment in bulk compared with shipment in barrels favoured the former to an annual amount of nearly £7000 per annum, equivalent to a saving on the delivered cost of oil of about £1 a ton.[18]

The first British-owned tanker was *Bakuin*, built by William Gray & Co, at West Hartlepool in 1886. With engines aft, fitted with electric light, she could carry 2000 tons dead weight at about 10 knots, and was built to the order of Alfred Suart under a 'cost-plus' building contract amounting to approximately £26000.

By the late 1880's and early 1890's there was a dramatic expansion in the sea carriage of petroleum with shipbuilders in North-East England playing the predominant part in perfecting the design of tonnage for the trade. Among early shipowners, we have already noted the enterprise of Alfred Suart, who owned 17 tankers of various designs by the mid-1890's, but when his fleet was valued, not all of his vessels were making a profit in the trade: Suart's fleet cost £652 626 but the net profit was only reckoned as £8726 in 1895, whereas James Knott's five 'Prince line' tankers cost £186 400 and earned £10 445. Despite these somewhat mixed fortunes, several other entrepreneurs entered the trade, among other J.M.Lennard of Middlesbrough, C.T.Bowring and Company of London, and most notably Marcus Samuel and Co of London, whose Anglo-Saxon Petroleum Company owned well over 30 ocean-going tankers in 1914, including two early diesel twin-screw vessels built by Palmers of Newcastle, with engines designed and manufactured in Amsterdam.

Several problems were encountered by the pioneers in this dynamically expanding but hazardous trade. The first of these related to the fact that petroleum increases in bulk as temperature rises, and the range of temperature encountered on passage was very considerable. An increase of temperature of $10°$ Fahrenheit increased the volume of the cargo by two per cent, so that the design of tanks for the carriage of petroleum had to allow for an amount of expansion (or contraction) during the voyage. Second, stability had to be ensured for a liquid cargo subject to surging when the ship encountered heavy seas and rolled or pitched as a consequence. This problem was reduced by the installation of a number of transverse bulkheads and a centre line bulkhead which divided the cargo into smaller parts so that surging was reduced. A trunk of small dimensions was added above each cargo tank, to which level the vessel was loaded: the space between the sides of the ship and the trunk could be then utilized for oil when the vessel was sailing on summer voyages when deeper loading was permissible. These 'summer tank' ships remained common until the 1930's when another expedient was adopted, namely, the addition of a second longitudinal bulkhead which effected further division of the tanks and further reduced

surging. This largely eliminated the need for the 'summer tank'. The many divisions now available, coupled with the increasing size of tankers, permitted the loading of a variety of grades of petroleum in the same vessel, thus increasing the flexibility of operations.

The third problem was to ensure proper ventilation both to reduce evaporation and to eliminate the risk of explosion when oil vapour and air created dangerous explosive gases. This hazard was responsible for several disastrous explosions in tankers, such as that which occurred at Newport, Monmouthshire, when *Tancarville* was in dry dock undergoing repairs in 1891.

Finally, there was the problem of ballasting. After the early years, during which several dry cargo ships were converted for the carriage of oil, it became the practice to construct most tankers with engines placed aft.[20] This reduced the risk of fire, and eliminated the need for a propeller shaft tunnel running beneath cargo tanks which could prove hazardous if there was the slightest leakage. But since oil tankers generally had long ballast passages, the weight of machinery aft necessitated these vessels having very elaborate ballast tanks so that optimal, efficient trim could be achieved.

Tankers built between the 1880's and 1910 were propelled by reciprocating steam engines, but in the latter year *Vulcanus* was built in Holland for the Anglo-Saxon Petroleum Company, and was notable as the first deep-sea motorship. Engined by the Werkspoor Company of Amsterdam, *Vulcanus*, a vessel of 1179 tons gross, with a deadweight of 1200 tons demonstrated the economy and reliability of diesel propulsion. With a speed of just over $6\frac{1}{4}$ knots, she was by no means a fast ship, but she proved exceptionally economical in the use of fuel: between 1911 and December 1921 she ran 307 528 miles on an average daily consumption of no more than 1.7 tons.

However, for many tankers steam was preferred, especially double reduction geared turbines, with correspondingly high pressure boilers.

Eagle Oil Transport Company initiated a major building programme of what were regarded as very large tankers – up to 16 000 tons deadweight – on the eve of the First World War, expressly for the transport of petroleum from the rapidly expanding Mexican oilfields. These vessels were equipped with quadruple expansion engines to give a service speed of between 10 and 11 knots, and were designed to burn oil fuel or coal – cheap oil fuel on the homeward leg from Mexico and coal on the return ballast passage. Subsequently, these vessels used oil fuel only, for which Anglo-Mexican Petroleum Products had waged a systematic and successful campaign. The commissioning of such large vessels was at first thought a risky experiment, but experience showed them to be exceptionally efficient vessels capable of transporting oil at lower cost than their smaller competitors. The full economies of scale in the transport of oil has reached its peak only in our own day, but there were portents for the future in the tankers designed in the 1920's and 1930's, with an increasing number of tanker owners specifying diesel propulsion. However, the exigencies of the Second World War saw the adoption of turbo-electric power in American standard tanker, the T2, introduced in the 1940's and one of the most successful merchant ship types ever produced.

The shipment of metallic ores posed problems of a different kind, but these were made apparent at an earlier stage in the development of the steamship than was the case with petroleum. Copper and iron ore were two exceptionally heavy cargoes which early attracted the attention of steamship owners: both trades had employed iron screw steamers from the late 1840's, but voyages were short and no particular problems were encountered except that stowage was a matter which required the exercise of great care, as the cargo took little space in the ship, and the weight was concentrated low in the hold, rendering the vessel liable to rapid and violent rolling in heavy seas, endangering masts and superstructure.

Despite this characteristic, much of the rapidly expanding trade in iron ore from ports such as Bilbao in Spain from the early 1870's was undertaken in common tramp steamers not especially adapted for the trade, since most owners wished to avoid limiting their employment to this one activity.

Specialized ships for the carriage of large quantities of ore were developed to a peak of efficiency on the inland waters of the Great Lakes in America, but shipbuilders in Britain constructed vessels that applied the lessons learned in America to European conditions. This was particularly true of the growing Swedish iron ore trade in the 1880's and 1890's. *Gellivara*, designed and built by C.S.Swan and Hunter, Newcastle in 1888 for Angier Line, London, was designed expressly for the new iron ore trade from Luleå in the Gulf of Bothnia. Of 2608 tons gross, her deadweight capacity was 3300 tons on a draught of no more than 17 feet. With twin screws she accommodated 12 first class passengers, and had topside wing tanks to achieve an effective trim. She was equipped with electric light and had two 20-ton derricks for handling cargo.

When Swedish ore was provided with a rail outlet to Narvik in North Norway, a number of ordinary tramp steamers entered that trade but although loading at that fine natural harbour posed no particular problems, discharge, at a range of Continental and British ports, by manual labour was extremely laborious and slow. The Johnson–Welin system was therefore adopted by one ship owner, in which ore was carried in bins or hoppers of iron built into the ship and placed athwartships, having sloping bottoms and equipped with suitable outlets. Discharge was

Gellivara, built of steel in 1888 by C.S.Swan & Hunter, Newcastle, was an early deep-sea iron ore carrier. Built to carry ore from Sweden she could load 3300 tons on a draught of 17 feet 4 inches. She incorporated wing tanks for the better stowage of an extremely heavy cargo which subjected the hull to exceptional strain.

Vollrath Tham was built by Hawthorn, Leslie & Co Ltd, Newcastle, in 1909 for the iron ore trade, and, with electric cranes, she could effect her own discharge. This plan differs in some respects from the builders' drawings preserved in the National Maritime Museum, but shows the essential detail of a ship which was revolutionary in her day, which has much in common with a modern bulk carrier. *Vollrath Tham* was built for Swedish owners, with a gross tonnage of 5846 and a deadweight capacity of 8000 tons.

mechanical, the vessels built under this system being equipped with an array of electric cranes powered by an electrical generating plant installed in the engine room of the ship. Two vessels were built embodying these design features in 1909 and 1910, both by R. and W.Hawthorn, Leslie and Co, of Hebburn-on-Tyne. *Vollrath Tham*, 8000 tons deadweight, was the first of these and *Sir Ernest Cassel* was the second – an even larger vessel, carrying 10800 tons dead-weight – the largest single-decked vessel engaged in ocean trade in her day. With all cranes working, each vessel could effect discharge in about 36 hours: had *Vollrath Tham* been equipped with ordinary steam winches, her discharge would have required about 40 hours. However, the big saving was in labour: about 120 men would have been required under the old method, whereas only 20 men were necessary for the new.

Vessels such as these were pioneers in the achievement of economies of scale and the adoption of labour-saving devices to secure rapid turn-round at low cost. Notable in this advance were *Amerikaland* and *Svealand* built with engines aft for the ore trade

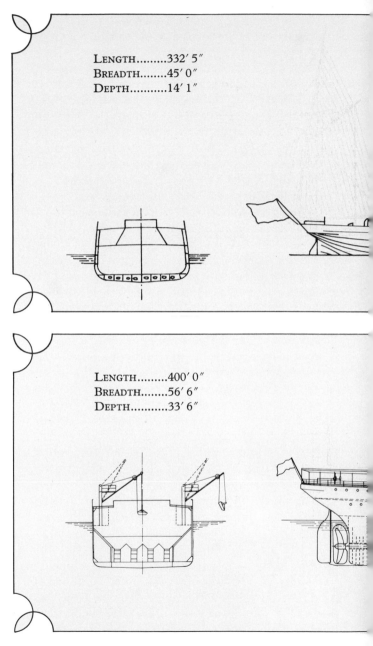

LENGTH.........332′ 5″
BREADTH.........45′ 0″
DEPTH...........14′ 1″

LENGTH.........400′ 0″
BREADTH.........56′ 6″
DEPTH...........33′ 6″

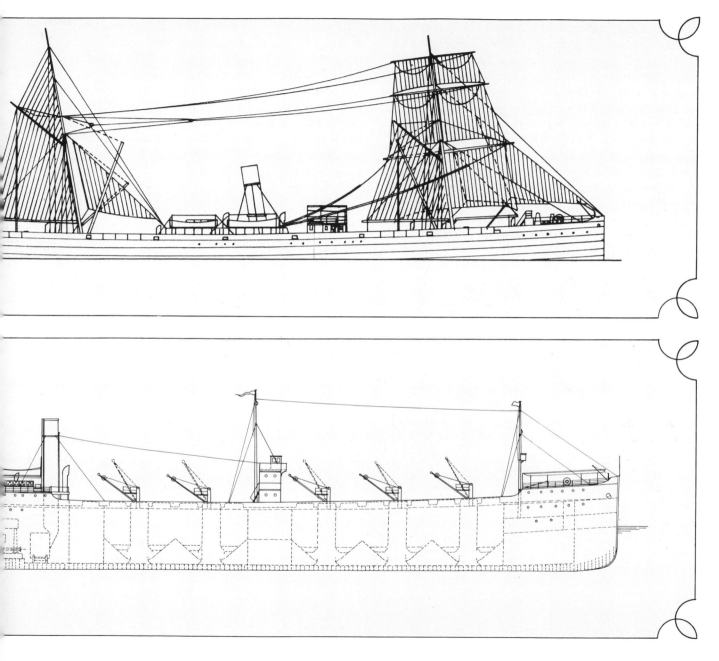

between Chile and either New Jersey or Baltimore. With a deadweight tonnage of 20 600 tons, and built and engined in Germany in 1925, these two extremely large, diesel-propelled vessels were in many respects the precursors of the modern bulk carrier. With large hatchways to facilitate rapid loading and discharge, these Swedish-owned ore carriers were among the first vessels to be fitted with steel hatchcovers. They could maintain a speed of 11¼ knots when fully loaded, on a daily consumption of 19½ tons. Routed through the Panama Canal they could make the voyage from Cruz Grande, Chile to Baltimore in under 19 days, and quick turn round time was assured as they could discharge a full cargo in no more than 16 or 18 hours.

Although rapid loading and discharge was a factor in the successful deployment of bulk carriers of this type, for the cargo liner there were different stowage problems, which manifested themselves with the advent of scheduled general cargo services from the 1860's onwards. Britain's import and export trade embraced an enormously wide range of miscellaneous goods in consignments of every conceivable size and consigned to an ever widening range of destinations in all the countries of the world:

Huge locomotives and railway bridges, marine boilers of unearthly form and immense weight, with butts of oil and bales of our finest fabrics, scrap-iron and cases of delicate instruments or works of art, agricultural engines and millinery, sulphuric acid and confectionery, lucifer matches

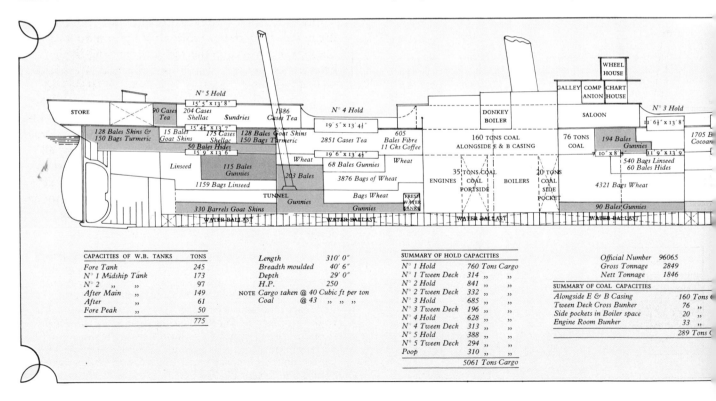

CAPACITIES OF W.B. TANKS	TONS
Fore Tank	245
N° 1 Midship Tank	173
N° 2 ,, ,,	97
After Main ,,	149
After ,, ,,	61
Fore Peak ,,	50
	775

Length	310' 0"
Breadth moulded	40' 6"
Depth	29' 0"
H.P.	250
NOTE Cargo taken @ 40 Cubic ft per ton	
Coal @ 43 ,, ,, ,,	

SUMMARY OF HOLD CAPACITIES		
N° 1 Hold	760	Tons Cargo
N° 1 Tween Deck	314	,, ,,
N° 2 Hold	841	,, ,,
N° 2 Tween Deck	332	,, ,,
N° 3 Hold	685	,, ,,
N° 3 Tween Deck	196	,, ,,
N° 4 Hold	628	,, ,,
N° 4 Tween Deck	313	,, ,,
N° 5 Hold	388	,, ,,
N° 5 Tween Deck	294	,, ,,
Poop	310	,, ,,
	5061	Tons Cargo

Official Number	96065
Gross Tonnage	2849
Nett Tonnage	1846

SUMMARY OF COAL CAPACITIES	
Alongside E & B Casing	160 Tons
Tween Deck Cross Bunker	76 ,,
Side pockets in Boiler space	20 ,,
Engine Room Bunker	33 ,,
	289 Tons C

and gunpowder, in short, something of everything 'to eat, drink and avoid', and all of these, say 2000 tons to be crowded into the hold of a ship of 1000 tons register.[21]

Since many liner services, as they developed from the 1860's and 1870's involved multi-port loading and discharge, there were complex problems of cargo assembly, loading, stowing, discharging and consigning to ultimate receivers. So far as ship design was concerned liner services often employed ships with two or more decks as circumstances dictated, and had to make elaborate arrangements to ensure that parcels of freight for one destination were not overstowed by consignments to be delivered at a port to be visited later in the scheduled itinerary. This was not all, however, since many individual con-

signments had characteristics which necessitated separate stowage, either because of the possibility of taint, or adulteration or because of particular hazards arising from noxious odours, vapours and the like.

It was not only the customer who had to be protected: the ship had, of course, to be loaded in accordance with the requirements of her intended itinerary, and it was not just a matter of ensuring that compatible consignments were stowed together. Regard had to be paid to the sailing qualities of the vessel, with matters of trim, stability and weatherliness constantly borne in mind. The typical stowage plan of a liner in the 1890's therefore, is a document that forms an essential, although often neglected, aspect of the typical liner operation as it developed in the second half of the 19th century.

One other new trade deserves mention since it illustrates both the increasingly diverse nature of oceanic commerce in the 19th century and the growing tendency towards specialization of function. Rising living standards in Britain and Europe had for long encouraged an expansion in the demand for meat, especially meat produced on the extensive grasslands of North and South America and Australasia. From the first, the steamship played no small part in the transport of live cattle carried coastwise around Britain, from Ireland, and, especially after 1844, from the Continent of Europe. With the advent of the relatively efficient oceanic cargo-carrying

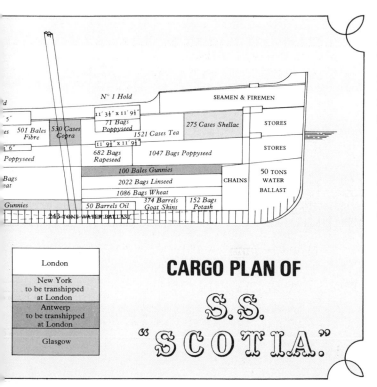

London

New York
to be transhipped
at London

Antwerp
to be transhipped
at London

Glasgow

CARGO PLAN OF

S.S.

"SCOTIA."

The liner trades often necessitated multi-port loading and discharge, as well as trans-shipments to other destinations not served directly. Such operations were expensive, and made more complicated the task of the shipowner, the stevedore and the docker. This typical stowage plan, taken from Captain H.Hillcoat's *Notes on the Stowage of Ships* (London, 1918), graphically illustrates the way in which heterogenous cargo consigned to different destinations was stowed on board one of 'Paddy' Henderson's homeward-bound liners from the Far East.

steamer a new trade was developed in live cattle across the Atlantic, from United States and Argentina, in which, for a hectic period, many ships were employed. Even before it had begun, however, the first tentative steps had been taken towards the perfection of a technique which was to supplant it. Methods of refrigeration were refined which permitted the installation of refrigerating machinery on board ships, and experiments were made in the 1870's especially by Charles Tellier, a Frenchman who had earlier invented an ammonia-absorption refrigerating apparatus. *Frigorifique*, formerly the African Steam Ship Company iron screw *Eboe* built at Liverpool in 1870, sailed from Rouen to Buenos Aires with a small consignment of meat, returning to Rouen after a voyage from Buenos Aires in 104 days with a much larger cargo not all of which arrived in good condition. However, a second Frenchman, Ferdinand Carré, who had perfected an ammonia-compression refrigeration machine, had one fitted in the steamship *Paraguay*, another ex-British built

screw steamer which had been built by Palmers and Co, at Jarrow in 1864. This vessel transported a cargo of 5500 carcasses of frozen mutton from San Nicolas consigned to Havre in 1877, but collision damage delayed her at St Vincent for no less than four months. Despite this misadventure, the meat was in good enough condition for the guests at the Grand Hotel in Paris to be fed on it for a whole week.

The British initiative in the shipment of frozen meat followed close on the heels of the successful disposal of *Paraguay's* cargo in France. Andrew McIlwraith chartered the steamship *Strathleven* from that highly enterprising Glasgow ship-owning firm of Burrell and Son, and she was fitted with a Bell-Coleman refrigerating unit in 1879. Loaded in Sydney and Melbourne with 40 tons of beef and mutton, she arrived in London in February 1880: a carcass of lamb was sent to Queen Victoria, and a sheep to the Prince of Wales.

Although some firms, such as Houlder Brothers, ventured into the meat trade, it was some time before

The fruit trade developed rapidly in the early 20th century, and the carriage of bananas was the principal business of Elders & Fyffes Ltd, who ordered *Pacuare* from Workman, Clark & Co Ltd of Belfast in 1905. Seen here in the harbour of Kingston, Jamaica, the island and the typical schooners form an attractive background to the white-hulled 'banana boat' which had a gross of 3891 tons and accommodation for passengers.

it was established on a regular basis. From 1890, however, the trade grew rapidly, and by December 1902 there were 147 vessels engaged in the frozen meat trade, having an aggregate capacity of 8 277 400 carcasses, and a further 10 vessels were being insulated or being built for the trade, with an additional capacity of 852 000 carcasses. By 1912, 218 vessels were engaged in carrying frozen meat, with a carrying capacity of 15 963 200 carcasses, equal to $17\frac{3}{4}$ lbs of meat for every man, woman and child in the United Kingdom. Refrigerated vessels were also employed in carrying dairy products, citrus fruit and bananas.

Refrigerated vessels, of which *Oswestry Grange* is a representative example, were faster than average: 12- to 14-knot ships were common, because of the perishable nature of the cargo and the expense involved in keeping the refrigerating machinery operating. They were also expensive to build and to equip with the necessary insulation: *Ovingdean*

Grange, built in 1890 for Houlder Brothers of London, 2413 tons, had Hall's system of refrigeration installed at a cost of £11 000 in 1895. Her capacity was 45 to 50 000 sheep carcasses, and she steamed 10 knots on 18 tons of coal per day, consuming an additional 3 tons per day for her refrigerating plant. The same shipowner chartered *Southern Cross* from Messrs. Wincott, Cooper and Co, built 1892, 5050 tons, which was fitted with refrigerating plant and insulated in 1896, at a cost of £17 000 (a sum that would have purchased a fair-sized tramp steamer); she steamed at 13 knots and earned £6000 nett profit in 6 months' trading in 1896.

Such vessels were all in regular liner trades and their speed and itineraries made them particularly attractive to passengers who were an important additional source of income to shipowners who sought to increase earnings in what were costly and risky enterprises.

Ruahine, owned by the New Zealand Shipping Co, was a typical refrigerated steamship of her day, and is seen here on trials on the Clyde in 1891. Built by Denny of Dumbarton, she was as heavily rigged as a Brig despite her quadruple expansion engines and three double-ended boilers supplying steam at 180 lbs per square inch. She was also fitted with Howdens system of forced draught. Her gross tonnage was 6127, with over 200 000 cu feet of insulated space, and a total deadweight capacity of 6690 tons, carrying in addition 74 first class, 36 second class passengers and having further accommodation for emigrants. She achieved over $14\frac{1}{2}$ knots on her trials, and her final price was £115 840.

Rossetti was a typical cargo steamer of the mid-1890s. Built of steel at Sunderland by J.L. Thompson & Sons, for Frederick Bolton of London, she measured 2080 tons gross. Seen here in the River Avon in a busy and characteristic setting, with hobblers boarding, a Severn trow ahead, and a steam tug astern.

Developments in the structure of cargo ships

Sir William White, speaking in 1906, said 'In no class of steamship has greater ingenuity and resource been shown than in the construction of the much maligned tramp steamer.'[22] He did no more than echo a distinguished predecessor, John Scott Russell who, in the middle of the 19th century, had asserted that the design and construction of cargo steamers posed more problems than any other kind of ship.

Among the main influences on the structure of the cargo ship in the second half of the 19th century were regulations brought in by the Marine Department of the Board of Trade with a view to securing adequate freeboard and the placing of a loadline so that ships were rendered safe at sea and the evils of overloading eliminated. At the same time, the principal classification organizations, especially Lloyd's Register of Shipping, also sought to secure safety at sea by standardizing what was thought best practice in construction, and by specifying detailed criteria, formulated the rules and regulations thought desirable to attain minimal risk to those who underwrote marine insurance policies. There were also significant modifications which derived from the efforts of the Board of Trade to regularize the measurement of the tonnage of ships in a uniform and equitable manner: in this, a covert war was waged by ingenious naval architects and shipowners who sought, not unnaturally, to secure maximum cargo capacity – of both weight and measurement goods – on the lowest possible registered tonnage. Because harbour and other dues were levied on registered tonnage, shipowners were anxious to minimize what for them was a significant proportion

of voyage costs, whilst, at the same time, dock and harbour authorities looked askance at shipowners' efforts to diminish the revenue derived from harbour tolls. Dock proprietors naturally sought to secure tonnage laws which would accurately reflect the actual capacity of vessels to carry cargo. This, then, is the background to any consideration of the developments in the structure of ships from the early 1850's.

Early screw steamers were in most respects very similar in configuration to the sailing ships they were destined gradually to supplant. They were mainly flush-decked, and consequently considerable care was required in loading and navigating if the safety of the ship was not to be prejudiced – this in the period before loadlines had been regularized. Flush-decked screw-propelled steamers could be navigated in conditions at sea in a manner which would have been impossible for sailing vessels, and could suffer the possibility of being swept from end to end by heavy seas. The chartering of screw colliers by the Transport Board for service to the Black Sea during the Crimean War necessitated alterations in these flush-decked vessels which often consisted of the erection of a monkey forecastle forward and a short poop aft. The monkey forecastle lessened the risk when encountering rough seas coming over the bow and afforded some protection to those working the anchors and accommodated forward, whilst a short poop aft provided shelter for the helmsman and to the hand steering gear, and helped to diminish the risks to which a following sea exposed the vessel. Amidships, a bridge house became a feature of ships built from the later 1850's, and some greater protection was accorded to the often flimsy glazed skylights and coverings to the engine and boiler spaces which were extremely vulnerable to a beam sea. The resultant profile in time evolved into the 'three island type' which was so familiar a feature of many tramp steamers from the 1870's.

As screw steamers increased in size to meet the growing demand of an expanding ocean commerce, the practical difficulty arose of maintaining the trim of the vessels, since the capacity of the after holds of ships with engines and boilers placed amidships was diminished by the propeller shaft and screw tunnel and by the need to fine the after end of the hull to produce a clean run to the screw propeller. To equalize the capacity of the fore and after hold spaces, the expedient adopted was to raise the deck from the after end of the engine-room bulkhead, and this raised quarter deck construction became an extremely safe and popular design for shipowners whose vessels were engaged in the carriage of bulk, homogeneous cargoes. North-East coast shipbuilders in particular adopted the forward well deck, and this was for many years a controversial innovation which was slow of acceptance by the Board of Trade, although the feature was proved to be both practical and safe.

For bulky cargoes of light merchandise, greater cubic capacity was desirable, and to meet this requirement poop, bridge and forecastle were often joined in a continuous structure forming spar or awning decks. Such designs were particularly suitable for the conveyance of passengers in the 'tween deck spaces thus created, and the awning deck vessels, with a light, well-ventilated structure, were utilized extensively in the pilgrim trades in Eastern waters. From the 1880's the live cattle trade across the Atlantic from America demanded a structure so that cattle could be accommodated in what came to be known as a shelter deck. The vessels incurred the wrath of Samuel Plimsoll, and committed him to a campaign not this time to protect human life as had been the case with his crusade for the load line, but to mitigate the suffering of cattle exposed to the wide, cold and often stormy waters of the North Atlantic. Shipowners did not wish to pay tonnage dues on what they regarded as temporary structures only suitable for cattle and not otherwise used for the stowage of cargo. To secure freedom from the increase in tonnage were these spaces to be permanently enclosed, ships were designed with tonnage openings before and abaft of the machinery spaces, with bulkheads for the purpose of protection, and portable hatches were used to cover these openings when vessels so designed proceeded to sea. Ultimately, the shelter deck was used increasingly for light general cargo, and while it remained technically 'open', it was not included in the calculations of registered tonnage.

These and other expedients were adopted to secure the shipowner the maximum economic advantage in the use to which he put his ship. He wanted to secure new tonnage as cheaply as possible, to minimize draught where he could, to increase his revenue earning potential and to reduce as far as he could his variable (voyage) costs. In achieving these ends in an intensely competitive market, he needed to compromise and, as one writer put it 'strike a judicious mean.'[23]

In the late 1850's Edward Harland of Belfast had built for Bibby of Liverpool the first in a series of iron screw steamers for the Mediterranean liner trade of exceptional length in proportion to beam, the ratio being as much as 10:1 in some cases. The reason for this was that it was then found that carrying capacity was increased thereby without any proportionate increase in the power of engines: thus fuel was conserved and freight earning potential was increased. A typical vessel of this type was the iron screw *Arabian*, built by Harland and Wolff, Belfast, for Bibby Line in 1862. She measured 335 feet in length, 34.2 feet in breadth, with a depth of 24.1 feet, on a gross tonnage of 2066. It was widely supposed by naval architects of that time that an increase in the beam of a steamship would necessarily increase the power needed to propel her at a given speed, but subsequently it was found that the extreme proportions of the type of vessel built for Bibby was not conducive to economy or carrying capacity. One of the most important theoretical verities, generally understood by the 1840's, was that the power necessary for a steam vessel increases according to the cube of her velocity. In other words, to double the speed of a steamship requires no less than eight times the power – or even more than that in the case of very fast vessels such as those built for the highly competitive Transatlantic passenger/emigrant trade. Considerations of this kind resulted in a divergence

'We did our best to fit up the *Egyptian*, *Dalmatian* and *Arabian* as first rate vessels', wrote Sir E.J.Harland of the Belfast shipyard Harland & Wolff. Built in 1862 to the order of Bibby Line of Liverpool, *Arabian* (pictured here) is a representative vessel of a type pioneered by the Belfast shipyard and the Liverpool shipowner, in which cargo carrying capacity was enhanced by adopting an increased length in proportion to beam, which, it was found, sacrificed little in speed. Of 1994 tons gross, *Arabian* measured 335 feet in length, 34 feet in beam and 25 feet in depth.

of practice between liners and tramps as they evolved in the following 20 or 30 years. Liner trades, particularly those to which passengers were a potential source of revenue, required fast ships, with all that was implied in prime cost, coal consumption and manning. For the tramp steamer, carrying bulk, homogeneous commodities, carrying capacity, draught and economy in coal consumption were the principal considerations, and it is readily understandable that speed was sacrificed in the interest of the other two variables. Thus the tramp of 1939 typically was only a knot or two faster than the tramp of 1870. Walter Runciman summarized in 1904 his long experience of tramp steamers when he pointed out that a typical 6000-ton tramp steamer would consume 20 tons of coal a day at 9 knots, 25 tons a day at 10 knots and 32 or 35 tons a day at 11 knots.[24]

The average size of the cargo steamer grew steadily from the 1860's onwards. By the mid-1880's, the typical merchantman was between 1500 to 2000 tons gross, and thereafter it grew almost every year, with very much larger ships being built in periods of greatest prosperity. Sometimes, as occurred between 1898 and 1901, it was feared that the larger tramp steamers coming into service would not suit the needs of merchants and charterers, and would be very limited in the range of ports to which they could trade by reason of their deeper draught, but, during the depression that ensued, it was the bigger tramps that best weathered the storm, so that these fears proved unjustified.

But the theory that extreme length was a commercial solution to increased cargo capacity was controverted by the experience accumulated by the builders of the large numbers of tramp steamers in

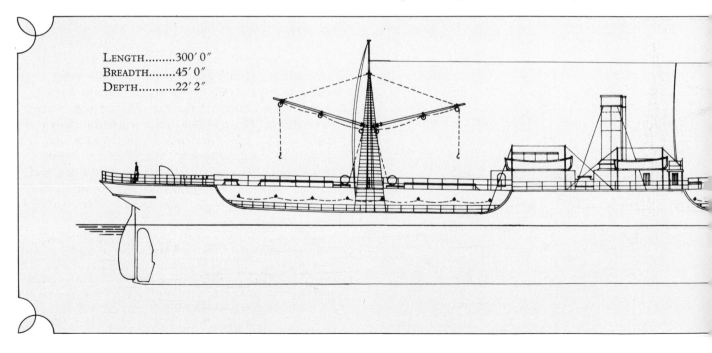

LENGTH.........300' 0"
BREADTH........45' 0"
DEPTH..........22' 2"

the 1870's and 1880's. Length was the most expensive dimension, and depth the cheapest, but increased depth implied increased draught, and draught was of critical importance in many trades. It was soon found that some increase in beam was a better way to achieve enhanced deadweight, but beam was of course constrained by the width of lock gates at many wet docks designed for the ships of an earlier period. Within limits, increased breadth did little to render steamships less economical, but, on the other hand, to carry comparable deadweight on less draught was more expensive in construction costs because more steel was required and the resultant heavier hull limited carrying capacity.

Considerations of space will not permit a detailed discussion of the many methods employed to achieve this 'judicious mean', but some developments require more than a passing mention, and reflect the

ingenuity and enterprise of designers and owners. Many of the new concepts were developed, it is worth noting, in times of recession or depression, when stringent economies were necessary in order to keep ships trading at any margin above their variable costs.

Among the innovations that proliferated between the 1900's and the 1920's were the Turret Deck and Trunk Deck cargo carriers designed and built by Messrs. Doxford and Messrs. Ropner respectively. These vessels owed not a little to American whale-back steamers, one of which visited Europe in 1892 and provoked great interest and discussion among naval architects and shipowners. Both types of vessel were essentially specialized bulk cargo carriers, especially suitable for homogeneous cargoes such as grain, coal or ore, but were less effective for the transport of bulky cargoes such as cotton. A large number of vessels were built to these designs and some shipowners ordered a whole succession of them, notably Cayzer, Irvine and Co, founders of the celebrated firm of Clan Line. The particular advantage of these designs was that strength was maximized, permitting the construction of larger bulk carriers, at a time when the size of the tramp steamer was particularly important, since it was found that larger vessels were much more economical in the propelling power necessary for a given speed than smaller ones. To the advantage of increased size and strength was added the diminution in the amount of steel work necessary to construct them. This effective

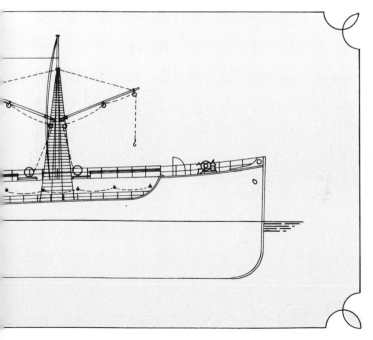

Trunkby was the first trunk-decked steamer and was both built and owned by a long-established firm of shipowners who became shipbuilders, Robert Ropner & Co, of West Hartlepool, who launched her from their Stockton shipyard in 1896. With triple expansion engines by Blair & Co Ltd of Stockton, she was a 4100-ton deadweight tramp steamer, of economical design. She was sunk by U-boat gunfire off Minorca in 1916.

The second of the Doxford-designed turret deck steamers was *Turret Age*, built in 1893 for Petersen, Tate & Co of Newcastle, who were the first shipowners to adopt this novel concept. The photograph gives a clear view of the hull configuration of this first turret deck design which had the machinery space placed aft. *Turret Age* is seen here discharging overside into a Humber keel.

Arcwear was built by Short Brothers Ltd of Sunderland in 1933 to the design of Sir Joseph W. Isherwood who developed his 'arcform' hull in order to achieve improvements in the stability, economy and efficiency of cargo ships. *Arcwear* could load 7068 tons of deadweight cargo on a loaded draught of 22 feet $7\frac{1}{2}$ inches. Propelled by triple expansion engines constructed by North Eastern Marine Engineering Co Ltd, the designed engine output was 1750 IHP with steam pressure at 220 lbs per square inch. On her maiden voyage she carried 6666 tons of coal and bunkers loaded at Immingham before undergoing measured mile trials off Polperro, after which she demonstrated her qualities by steaming from Plymouth to Buenos Aires at an average speed of 10.64 knots on a daily consumption of 19.55 tons of coal.

saving of weight enhanced their carrying capacity. The turret ship gave a $6\frac{1}{2}$ per cent superior deadweight capacity compared with a comparable conventionally built single-deck steamer. Another advantage was that deadweight was increased in relation to net tonnage – by as much as 8 per cent on the same comparison.

Another design to achieve some success was the 'corrugated' ship, introduced by Osbourne, Graham and Co, Sunderland with *Monitoria*, 1904 tons gross, built in 1909 for Ericsson Shipping Co, of Newcastle-upon-Tyne. This type, too, required less power for a given speed, had very favourable stability and freedom from excessive rolling. *Monitoria* could carry about 6 per cent more cargo than her conventionally constructed contemporary.

A highly influential design was introduced by Joseph W. Isherwood, who had been trained at Furness, Withy and Co's West Hartlepool shipyard, and who left his work as surveyor to Lloyd's Register in order to promote his own design of longitudinal framing. This system, which owed much to a concept introduced by John Scott Russell half a century earlier, also had the advantage of saving the weight of steel used in construction, by as much as 10 per cent, permitting the shipowner to enjoy increased

deadweight capacity without any corresponding increase in draught. The new system was found particularly appropriate in the construction of tankers and the first vessel built under it was the tanker *Paul Paix* in 1908. She was of somewhat unusual design apart from her constructional novelties, since she had machinery space amidships. The Isherwood system was by far the most influential design and tankers even today still owe a great deal to this form of construction. In the 1930's, Isherwood again proved an innovator, when he introduced the 'Arc form' ship, of which *Arcwear* was the first. Built by Short Brothers Ltd of Sunderland in 1930, with machinery installed by North Eastern Marine Engineering Co Ltd, she showed remarkable economy in coal consumption whilst maintaining an excellent speed and admirable stability.

Earlier, yet another system which enjoyed some success was developed by Ayre and Ballard, and their design was embodied in the screw steamer *Edenor* completed in 1912. The designers claimed that this 'Arch' system of shipbuilding as it was called, gave 18 per cent less weight of materials than conventionally constructed cargo steamers of equivalent deadweight and speed. Some 26 vessels were built to this system.

The iron screw *Glenfruin* officially opened London's
Tilbury Dock on 17 April 1886, towed through the old
entrance lock by two typical London twin-funnelled paddle
tugs. In the foreground of an animated scene is the steam
launch *Useful*. *Glenfruin* was a typical general cargo carrier
of the 1880s, built by the London & Glasgow Company on
the Clyde. She measured 2985 tons gross, was rigged as a
barque with compound inverted engines working at a
pressure of 80 lbs per square inch, and was owned by
McGregor, Gow & Company who employed her in the Far
Eastern trades.

Commercial organisation and the freight market

Liner companies could, to some extent, protect themselves from short-run fluctuations in costs, more particularly if they participated in one or other of the shipping 'conferences' which proliferated from the mid-1870's. However, no such stability could be assured for the tramp sector in which the market was close to being perfect. Because of the large number of individual tramp ship companies, the international nature of the freight market (the Baltic Exchange in London being unrivalled in its scope, flexibility and competence) and the presence in London and other major British ports of a wide spectrum of owners' and charterers' brokers, the freight rates prevailing were subject to extreme, and, to the outsider, often bewildering changes. As one writer put it '. . . from every port and on every line of traffic, the rates are constantly changing in a way which would stagger a railway traffic manager.'[25] It follows from this that the profitability of the tramp steamer was similarly subject to marked fluctuations: short-lived years of prosperity were inevitably followed by dramatic and often prolonged periods of depression from which recovery was protracted. Nevertheless, there is some evidence to suggest that well-managed tramp shipping enterprises could contrive a better return on capital invested than was available to many liner companies. Fixed costs for tramps were small, but for liners they were very considerable. Voyage costs for liners were also higher than for tramps, but they could cream off many of the better paying freights, and the quantity of cargo offered to liners was less subject to marked variation than those bulk freights in which the tramp

specialized, since the latter depended critically upon such random factors as harvest conditions around the world. Variable, or voyage, costs were the most significant element in total costs for the tramp, and such tonnage would continue to trade so long as these costs were more or less covered. The only alternative to keeping ships employed and hoping for better things was for the tramp ship owner to lay up one or more units in his fleet. But laid up shipping always posed a threat to any recovery in freight-rates that might be forthcoming, since the recommissioning of vessels in any considerable numbers could rapidly glut the market.

Periods of depression were the times when the marginal, inexperienced or incompetent tramp shipowner would be forced out of business, while prudent managers who had accumulated contingency reserves or who had depreciated the value of their tonnage realistically, could expect to survive all but the most persistent storms. Not a few of the most celebrated tramp shipowners, such as Burrell or Furness, were to be found ordering new tonnage when shipyards were nearly idle, securing exceptionally cheap vessels, often purchased under cost price, from shipbuilders anxious for the future and desperate to maintain some continuity of employment for their skilled hands. Thus shrewd shipowners not only secured tonnage more cheaply, but it was often better constructed because the work was better done, and delivery dates were reduced so that return on the capital outlay was quickly forthcoming. Furthermore, shipbuilders were often prepared to offer exceptionally favourable financial terms to prospective purchasers, frequently participating in the ownership of the vessels they built thus reducing yet again the capital outlay. The exigencies of low freights were often instrumental in the promotion of cost-reducing innovations in design or machinery, so that the owner could embody in his new ships the latest improvements. Such exceptionally efficient tonnage would stand the shipowner in good stead since he could undercut his rivals and stood ready to benefit once a revival of the market manifested itself.

Market recovery was often the signal for feverish speculation in the purchase of tonnage, both new and secondhand. There would follow a hectic period of rising prices and delivery dates would be prolonged. Ships would be less carefully built and 'enterprising nobodies'[26] would flock into shipowning intoxicated by the prospect of a boom. However, the gap between equilibrium and an overstocked freight market was exceptionally narrow. As delivery dates lengthened the speculator could well find himself launched into shipowning with new tonnage just as the freight market's upward surge had begun to falter or decline. A flood of tonnage released on a fully stocked market would precipitate a rapid declension in rates, and the passive investors who had been so eager to participate in shipping investment a few months earlier would be reluctant to commit capital in the face of uncertain prospects. Then many speculative, transient, ship-owning enterprises would founder on the rocks of unfulfilled expectations.

Despite the hazards endemic in tramp shipowning, there was no shortage of recruits to the industry, especially from the early 1870's when entrepreneurs, particularly in North-East England, began to devote a great deal of capital to this form of investment. Such ports as Sunderland, the Hartlepools, New-castle, North Shields and Whitby rapidly acquired fleets of ships which were to form the nucleus of substantial and long-lived maritime enterprises.

Not a few such firms established branch offices in London, or Cardiff so that they enjoyed the benefits of proximity both to the London freight market and to the focus of the overseas coal trade which was largely centred in the Welsh port. To secure good charters or contracts of coal from Wales was not infrequently the essential basis for profitable enterprise.

The typical tramp of the 1870's was about 1000 to 1200 tons gross, costing around £16 000 to £20 000. This kind of tonnage was generally owned under the '64th' system, with subscribers paying about £250 or £300 for 1/64th share in a new vessel. Typically, the shares were widely distributed, with managing owners ('ship's husbands') holding upward of 4/64ths, the remaining shares being held most often by ten or fifteen individuals. In the early 1870's – prosperous years for the shipping industry – dividends could be as high as 40 per cent on the capital subscribed, although 20 to 25 per cent was a more common return. These 'sixty-fourthers' were share-holders in ships which they held with unlimited liability – they received dividends in accordance with the earnings of the ship, but they correspondingly incurred liabilities for debts, including (for example) heavy repairs or replacements, or for such eventuali-ties as collision. Although these shareholdings were widely spread, they comprised a rather limited group of individuals who would invest in a considerable number of different vessels. Most of them had economic interests in the North-East or North-West of England, and most were prepared to repose con-siderable confidence in the individual or firm designated as managing owner. With the efflux of time, shares would become more widely distributed among a more disparate number of individuals, as shares were quite readily bought and sold, and could be almost equally readily mortgaged, although joint-stock banks in some parts of Britain took more kindly to loans against such security than did others. It was often alleged that banks were a major factor in some parts of Britain (e.g. the North-East and Cardiff) in contributing to the instability of the freight market by too readily granting credit both to shipbuilders seeking new orders, ship managers and, particularly, the more or less passive investors.

Ownership of vessels under the '64th' system was appropriate for ships of modest size and capital cost and in which the shareholders had some identity of interest. The advent of the big liner company, and limited liability, however, had important consequences for the structure of shipping firms, and permitted substantial fleets of ships to be organized under the changing laws that regulated joint stock companies in the 19th century. So far as the large joint stock companies formed to operate mail or passenger services were concerned, their first

Whitby was a small north-east coast seaport with interests in shipping, shipbuilding and the Fisheries out of all proportion to its size. Both shipowning and shipbuilding are represented in this photograph of the steel screw steamer *Trongate*, built by Thomas Turnbull at his Whitehall shipyard, Whitby in 1897 for the associated firm Turnbull, Scott & Co. With triple expansion engines manufactured by Blair & Co of Stockton, she measured 2553 tons and was typical of the vessels built for this long-established British shipowner. The building of the steel screw steamers ended at Whitby early this century because of the limitation on the size of ship imposed by the narrow opening of Whitby Bridge.

requirement was for very considerable funds so that they could build fleets of ships large enough to maintain regular services: this was especially true of those enterprises, such as Cunard, Royal Mail Steam Packet Co, Pacific Steam Navigation, or Peninsular and Oriental which aspired to procure government subventions for the carriage of mail. Some of these enterprises obtained Royal Charters, and most assumed joint stock company status, permitting them to appeal to a wide range of investors by issuing shares or stock. With the advent of limited liability, these firms assumed that character, and investors received dividends on their shares according to the profitability or otherwise of the fleet, rather than the individual vessel, as was the case under the '64th' system. Given the heavy capital investment not only in fleets of large ships, but also in costly shore establishments necessary to ply their trade, it was not surprising that these liner firms showed a distinct tendency towards mergers and amalgamations, especially in the 20th century under the systematic and pervasive influence of the 'conference' system.

For smaller individual enterprises, however, limited liability provided the opportunity to establish what came to be called the single-ship company, a phenomenon that embraced both sailing vessels and steamers, particularly from the 1870's until the First World War, although there was a powerful reaction against the trend early in the present century.

One motive for the adoption of this structure of ownership was to limit liability for collision damage, but another was simply the convenience of operating tonnage thus, especially when the cost of ships (because of their increasing size) made the division of the tonnage into 64ths unwieldy, or limited the range of prospective investors because the individual share was too large to encourage the smaller investor who was to prove an important source of capital in the later 19th century. The majority of ships owned under this system were nominally independent companies, but in fact linked by ship managers who would direct the fortunes of a considerable fleet. The majority of these managers were highly respectable shipowners of tremendous experience, not a few of whom survived as household names in the world of shipping well into the present day. But the system was abused by some unscrupulous individuals who launched fraudulent single-ship firms and deceived unsuspecting and ignorant investors, who were

attracted (when times were prosperous) by the promised riches implicit in the 40 per cent dividends claimed as being earned by tramp steamers. Abuses of the system could have a marked effect on the whole shipping industry, especially when injudicious investment in new tonnage threatened the stability of the freight market (as it did in the 1880's), or when made desperate by miscalculation, managers were found to be over-insuring their ships in the expectation of their foundering at sea, or gambling in the marine insurance on ships in which they had no pecuniary interest beyond that of encouraging that expectation in others.

Okhla was a fine steel cargo vessel built by William Denny & Brothers of Dumbarton for the British India Steam Navigation Co in 1895. Seen here on her trials on the River Clyde, she achieved a speed of $11\frac{1}{2}$ knots, although designed to steam at 10 knots with a cargo of 8040 tons on a draught of 24 feet 6 inches. The price to her owners was £52 762 on which Denny made a profit of £4227. She was a casualty in the First World War, being mined in 1917.

The diminutive *Tivyside* of Cardigan, seen here in the River
Avon in the 1890s, was built on the Clyde in 1869 for
Cardigan owners. Originally she measured 105 tons gross,
before being lengthened by 15 feet at Liverpool in 1896 for
her final owner John Bacon of Liverpool. Little cargo
steamers of this kind played an important, but neglected,
part in the coasting trade of Britain in the 19th century.
Tivyside was wrecked near Port Eynon, Gower Coast in
1900.

The coasting and short-sea trades

The coasting trade of Britain from 1850 was by no means dominated by the steamship, but it played an increasingly important rôle, slowly ousting the sailing ship from the more profitable traffic. Sail was driven into the marginal trades where speed in transit was of less importance, and to ports or harbours where the volume of commerce was insufficient to sustain the installation of expensive cargo handling equipment at the quayside. Some cargoes remained the mainstay of sailing ships because of the protracted time needed to load and discharge them. One instance of this was the slate trade of North Wales, which was of importance in the decision of shipowners in ports such as Porthmadog to prolong investment in new sailing vessels well into the 20th century because the handling of such cargoes was of necessity a long and tedious process. The capital and running costs of small sailing vessels being much less than steamers of equivalent size, they were best adapted to those trades which involved lengthy delays, since demurrage charges on the vessel were almost negligible. However, even such traditional trades as that in slate saw the incursion of the coastal steamship by the beginning of the present century. The sailing vessel was consigned to increasingly peripheral transport of bulky, low value, homogeneous freights such as coal, fertilisers, feeding-stuffs and china clay – these were typical consignments that sustained the declining and ageing fleet that constituted the last survivors of a glorious era. During, and especially just after, the First World War, the owners of many of these vessels found that the installation of auxiliary engines – mainly of the hot-bulb type, became a necessity for survival in the depressed 1920's and 1930's. Somehow, a few of these craft contrived to eke out a livelihood for their owners and crews well into the 1950's.

The steam coasting trade may be divided into three main sectors, with a great deal of interchange between them. First, there were the vessels almost exclusively devoted to the carriage of coal – partly for household or industrial use, but more especially for use in gas works and (later) electricity generating stations. Such tonnage was, as we have seen, almost the first to demonstrate the advantages of iron hull construction allied with the screw propeller. The size of the screw collier steadily increased as port authorities began to improve their facilities, and the depth of water was increased by the advent of a different kind of steam vessel – the dredger. Thus economies of scale were achieved in this sector as in others as the century progressed: larger ships were designed and incorporated more efficient means of loading and discharge. In this, efficiency was increased by investment in heavy working gear by substantial firms specializing in the purchase and redistribution of coal such as William Cory & Sons in London who were owners of an important collier fleet. In 1860 they acquired a floating derrick, originally constructed by the Thames Iron Shipbuilding Co in 1859 to raise sunken wrecks. This vessel, in the form of an elongated hexagon, measured 250 feet long by 90 feet wide. Fitted with six hydraulic cranes, *Atlas*, as she was called, could effect the discharge of a 900-ton deadweight collier in six hours directly overside into barges and lighters. This had a marked effect on the turn-round time of the steam collier and reduced the congestion created by the 'bunching' of colliers in the river. So successful was *Atlas* that another floating derrick was commissioned, named *Atlas II*, and the original vessel was renamed *Atlas I*. In 1875 the two floating derricks together discharged $1\frac{1}{4}$ to $1\frac{1}{2}$ million tons of the $2\frac{3}{4}$ million tons of coal imported to London by sea.[27]

Some collier owners acquired tonnage of a specialized design to meet the requirements of particular ports or customers. One example was the collier type nick-named the 'flatiron' which was evolved to carry

coal up the Thames above bridges to serve gas works (and later, power stations) on the upper reaches of the river. 'Flatirons' were constructed with a marked absence of fore and aft sheer and were given lowering masts and funnels, thus earning them their name. In 1884, the Hartlepool shipbuilders E.Withy & Co launched the 'flatiron' *Vane Tempest* for the Marquis of Londonderry, who at this time had 13 screw colliers in the coal trade out of Seaham Harbour. Of 689 tons gross, *Vane Tempest* was followed in 1886 by three similarly constructed colliers built by the neighbouring shipyard of William Gray & Co, at a cost of £33250. They were the iron screw vessels

'Despatch is the life of the coal trade' was a remark that emphasized the importance of securing the rapid loading and discharge of steam colliers. That most enterprising shipbuilding firm, William Doxford & Sons of Sunderland designed a self-discharging collier for Sauber Brothers of Hamburg which they patented in 1911. The steel screw

Herman Sauber, 2913 tons gross, was completed in 1912 and was fitted with a continuous conveyor self-discharging system which permitted the delivery of 400 tons of coal per hour on each side of the ship either to trucks or lighters, employing no more than seven men at a cost of less than one farthing per ton.

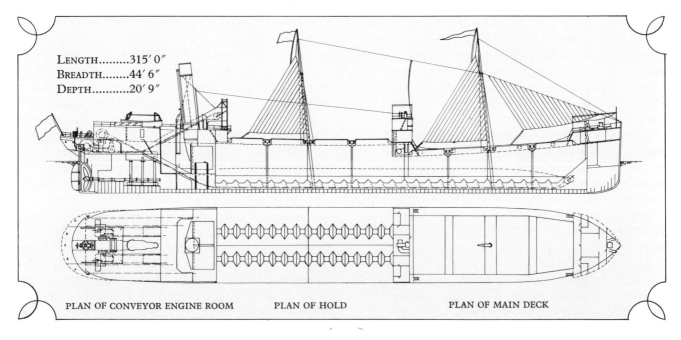

LENGTH........315' 0"
BREADTH........44' 6"
DEPTH..........20' 9"

PLAN OF CONVEYOR ENGINE ROOM   PLAN OF HOLD   PLAN OF MAIN DECK

Stepney and *Wapping*, each 953 tons deadweight, and the steel screw *Poplar*, 1255 tons deadweight. The London Gas Light and Coke Company also acquired a considerable fleet of 'flatirons' to meet their needs, and these vessels became an extremely familiar sight on the river.

In the 1900's William Doxford & Sons Ltd of Sunderland patented a new type of collier in which the Hamburg firm of Sauber Brothers invested. These vessels were equipped with large self-trimming hatchways and holds of the hopper type with wing water-ballast tanks and a specially designed conveyor system so that the vessel could effect her own powered discharge through delivery shoots overside. Typical of such was *Emma Sauber* (launched as *Pallion*), a steel 2474 tons gross ship with engines placed aft, constructed in 1909.

The second category of coastal and short-sea steamship was the cargo liner which often combined the carriage of freight with passengers. Such shipping was deployed in more or less regular services, offering merchants and traders a schedule of rates, and accepting highly heterogeneous cargoes ranging from the common domestic necessaries to raw materials, semi-manufactures and finished products. Trans-shipment cargo from or for ocean liners berthed at the principal deep-sea ports was an important source of custom, particularly after the deep sea liner trade, organized in shipping conferences, established a world-wide network of regular foreign ports of call. Many regional industries in Britain relied heavily on such facilities as these coastwise liners provided: notably the tinplate industry of South Wales, which received tin and palm oil by these services, and took advantage of such ships to send tinplate to ports such as Liverpool and London from whence the ocean freighters sailed to a multitude of foreign destinations. These feeder services proliferated in the late 19th century despite fierce railway competition.

It is almost impossible to describe representative types of vessel engaged in the coastwise and short-sea liner trades as the vessels were notably heterogeneous in design and construction. Many were hardly distinguishable from the vessels that formed the third category of trader, the coastal tramps which superseded sailing vessels. They carried virtually any bulk cargo that required moving between British or the near Continental ports between Elbe/Brest limits, or occasionally, beyond. Few such vessels registered more than 1500 tons gross, since larger vessels were faced with severe constraints upon their employment, given the depth of water available in the numerous smaller British and European ports. It has been estimated that perhaps half of the total coastal fleet was engaged in the coal trade just before the First World War, so that the remaining two categories shared a considerable volume of traffic, and many ships were deployed in either form of activity at one time or another. John Masefield's 'Dirty British Coaster' was, from the poet's description of her cargo, more of a lady than a tramp.

The decline in Britain's coastal shipping that occurred between 1913 and 1921 has been described by one historian as an 'eclipse'.[28] This might perhaps be regarded by some as something of an exaggeration, but nonetheless there was a diminution in the volume of coastal trade and a consequential decline in the number of ships dependent on this activity. Many small firms of long standing ceased trading soon after the First World War. As was the case with deep-sea shipping, the coaster and short-sea trader was hard hit by the war: war-time casualties were heavy, and many firms emerged from the conflict with fleets much reduced in numbers. The building programme induced by the immediate post-war euphoria only partially restored the aggregate tonnage, and indeed, added to the problems in the profound depression that was to ensue.

There can be no doubt that railway competition played a significant part in this decline, especially was this the case after railways came under government control. Shipowners complained that railway rates were set at an unrealistically low level, particularly the port-to-port rates which were often 'exceptional' rates fixed with an eye to the challenge presented by sea transport. This discrimination affected both the important inter-port general cargo trade, and the coastwise transport of such regular staple freights as coal. A new trade, in petroleum products, only partly offset this decline in opportunities for shipowners in the coastwise and short-sea sector, but this highly specialized freight demanded tonnage which could not be adapted to alternative uses.

Princess Sophia (506 tons gross) was built as the *Topaz* in 1893 by Scott & Co, of Bowling, with engines by Muir & Houston, for William Robertson's Glasgow 'Gem Line'. She was soon afterwards sold to Langlands who renamed her and employed her in their coastal services from the Clyde. She was very typical of many steam coasters and short sea traders built between the 1890s and 1930s, and such vessels were ubiquitous in British and near-Continental ports for over two generations, until gradually displaced by diesel-engined coasters of modern design.

William France, Fenwick & Company have had a long experience in the operation of screw colliers, and *Holywood*, seen here in ballast trim in 1932 is representative of a large class of early 20th-century coal carriers. Built in 1907 by J. Blumer & Co of Sunderland, she had a single deck, and measured 1545 tons gross. In 1935 she passed to the Greek flag and was renamed *Tanais*.

Dalewood was built for William France, Fenwick & Co in 1931 by S.P. Austin & Son Ltd who specialized in the design and construction of colliers. With machinery aft, bridge amidships and four large hatches to facilitate the working of cargo, she was typical of the reciprocating-engined coal traders still being built for British owners in the 1930s.

Another source of increasing concern to shipowners in this field was of course, the growth of road haulage as the lorry became an alternative, cheap, quick and flexible method of moving consignments throughout Britain. Furthermore, the facilities offered by many ports did not always match the level of efficiency which would have retained for coastal shipping that part of aggregate freight carriage the industry rightly regarded as its fair share.

One response to declining profitability in coastal shipping, particularly in the liner trades, was amalgamation and take-over: numerous independent firms were absorbed by a new conglomerate, Coast Lines Limited, vigorously led by Sir Alfred Read, which assumed a dominant rôle in maintaining coastwise liner services. An enlightened shipbuilding programme gave new ships with the black funnel and white chevron a particular distinction in the 1930's especially, when diesel propulsion was widely adopted in an increasingly attractive fleet of vessels.

A feature of Britain's coasting and short-sea trades which had become noticeable in the pre-war period became even more prominent after the First World War. There was a marked incursion of foreign tonnage, especially Dutch, and, in the inter-war years, the Dutch motor coaster maintained an ubiquitous presence at almost every British port. There had been straws in the wind well before the war, however. Early in 1907 an iron three-masted schooner attracted much attention as she berthed at Teignmouth. With a straight stem and three short masts, which could be lowered, the vessel could pass up rivers to destinations as far inland as Cologne. With self-trimming hatches, winches and cargo-handling gear she could carry 335 tons deadweight on the very modest draught of 11 feet. Significantly, she required only a crew of six. Even more significantly, she was equipped aft with a 60-hp internal combustion engine, giving her a cruising speed, under propellers alone, of five knots. Such vessels

Coast Lines Ltd, of Liverpool, by a process of amalgamation assumed the dominant rôle in coastal liner services between British ports from the 1920s. A typical Coast Lines vessel was the motorship *Atlantic Coast*, built by Henry Robb Ltd at Leith in 1934, with diesel engines built by British Auxiliaries Ltd, of Glasgow. With twin screws and a shelter deck for the carriage of general cargo on scheduled services, she represented the finest type of British coaster of the 1930s. Her gross tonnage was 890, on dimensions 232 feet by 35 feet by 12 feet.

were the precursors of what in the inter-war years became a major threat to British short-sea and coastal shipowners, especially those engaged in the tramp sector. These Dutch coasters, light of draught, embodying diesel propulsion, cheaply financed, very economically manned, and combining exceptional deadweight capacity in relationship to tonnage, assumed an increasing threat to British shipowners who were sometimes slow to adapt their tonnage to new technological possibilities. There is an obvious parallel here with the situation in which the British cargo ship often found itself in the same inter-war period. However, the discriminatory railway rating system, the advent of road haulage and the indifferent facilities afforded by many British ports did little to engender confidence, even in the short run, among shipowners. The post-war depression, prolonged in its incidence and widespread in its effects on European commerce, redoubled the understandable anxieties, and many, even far sighted, shipowners could be forgiven for what might seem in retrospect excessive caution, though to contemporaries it must more often have been regarded as commercial prudence.

Most steam and motor coasters trading as colliers or tramps were raised quarter-deck vessels with a well deck forward, and bridge structure amidships. Most were fitted with engines aft: this obviated the need for a long shaft tunnel with the consequential reduction in cargo space. Furthermore hatches and hold were designed to be free from obstruction and this facilitated the speedy loading and discharge of cargo – a factor that naturally assumed particular importance to the short-sea shipowners who must reckon to have his vessel in port for longer than ships engaged in oceanic trade. The preponderant part of the coastal shipping fleet were vessels with two hatches or holds, one forward and one abaft the bridge, but smaller vessels with a single hold would have the bridge aft, whilst the larger vessels, especially the bigger types of collier would have three or four hatches, to facilitate rapid loading and discharge at well-equipped regular berths. Indeed, the self-trimming collier with large hatches became a requirement of the coal trade, as did vessels with unobstructed holds permitting the use of grabs, but grab damage was the source of perpetual problems for the shipowner. Light draught in relation to deadweight was especially important, as was ease in lying aground, since many of the small ports habitually traded to were tidal with poor layerage. For similar reasons, efficient cargo handling gear was a necessity if trade to ill-equipped ports was to be contemplated.

Speed was of no great consequence for such vessels and few required bunkers for more than three or four days' steaming under normal circumstances. Given that harbour and pilotage dues were levied on registered tonnage, and that such costs formed a significant proportion of voyage costs, there were material inducements for maximizing the carrying capacity of the vessel and securing the minimum net tonnage.

The coastal liners had most features in common with the tramps, but here shelter decks were often fitted in order to simplify the stowage problems for ships carrying heterogeneous cargoes often with multiple-port loading and discharge. A knot or two of extra speed above that required for the tramp ensured that schedules could be kept despite the incidence of bad weather: to reach port on the planned tide was often an essential prerequisite for optimal employment. Liner tonnage of this type was generally designed to have a relatively larger hold cubic capacity than was customary among the tramps or colliers so that they could accommodate bulky and light cargoes.

All these coastal and short-sea traders shared with

the deep-sea cargo vessel the full range of technical improvements as it influenced economy in engines and boilers. The vessels of the 1850's and 1860's still carried sails as an auxiliary source of power, and some shipowners persisted in carrying canvas into the present century. In the 1860's compound engines were almost invariably installed with boiler pressure at about 60 psi. By 1880 notable economies in coal consumption had been achieved. For example the iron screw steamer *Woodstock*, built that year by Messrs. Ramage & Ferguson of Leith, with compound engines constructed by Messrs. Fleming & Ferguson of Paisley, consumed 7 tons 12 cwts of Scotch coal per 24 hours, the equivalent of 2.37 lbs per indicated horse power. This vessel measured 593 tons gross, carried 600 tons of cargo and cost about £11000. Her engines indicated 300 hp and boiler pressure was 80 psi.[29] In later decades, boiler pressures were increased in accordance with the same

technological imperatives that determined the design of deep-sea fleets, with boiler pressures of 160–200 psi and triple expansion engines substituted for compound engines in the 1880's.

It has often been suggested that, in the inter-war years, shipowners in Britain were slow to adopt diesel propulsion despite the advocacy of such writers as A.C.Hardy and Walter Pollock. By the 1930's, however, several shipowners embraced the internal combustion engine with more enthusiasm, and derived the benefits that flowed from their commitment in meeting the challenge of the ubiquitous Dutch. Owners who were far-sighted enough were thus enabled to take full advantage of the recovery in freight rates that occurred in the years immediately before the Second World War. Not surprisingly, as the Dutch shipyards had developed considerable expertise in the building of these motor coasters, a number were purchased by

British steam coasters faced a challenge in the 1930s with the advent of large numbers of very economical, efficient motor vessels mainly built and owned in Holland. A few British shipowners, notably F.T.Everard & Sons and Coast Lines Ltd soon responded to the competition by ordering diesel-engined craft from British shipyards, while others such as Thomas J.Metcalf, placed orders with Dutch builders. A representative vessel was the Waterhuizen-built motor coaster *Polly M.* of 1937, 380 tons, a two hatch, well decker, pictured here in the River Thames, to which she habitually traded.

British shipowners, such as T.O.Metcalf, but the largest owners of motor coasters was the long established firm of F.T.Everard & Sons Ltd whose experience ranged over the whole spectrum of coastal shipping from Thames Spritsail barges to modern tankers. Everards were in the vanguard so far as the adoption of the diesel engine was concerned and built a large number of vessels in British shipyards, using diesel units mainly designed and manufactured by the Newbury Diesel Company or British Polar Atlas of Glasgow. The trend towards diesel propulsion was almost complete by 1939.

Comparative data concerning the typical coaster as it was developed between 1906 and the early 1950's may be summarized thus:

	Steam coaster of 1906	Motor coaster of 1953
No. of crew	17	17
Length bp	184.5 ft	199 ft
Beam	27.5 ft	34 ft
Depth	13.625 ft	15 ft
Draught	13.8 ft	14.6 ft
Displacement	1390	1989
Deadweight	805	1347
Speed on trial	10[1]	11[3]
Cargo capacity (cu ft)	32 400	68 190
Bunkers (tons)	70	75
Engines	Comp. Surf. Cond.	Polar 6 cylinder
Power	774 (IHP)	1100 (BHP)
Consumption per day (tons)	17	5

These figures suggest the superior efficiency achieved by the motor coaster of the 1950's compared with her early 20th-century counterpart. With the same crew, the 1950 motor vessel carried 542 tons more deadweight cargo, and doubled her cubic capacity, so that she was better adapted for a wider range of possible freights, especially those of a bulky nature. In addition to these advantages, the diesel-propelled motor coaster had a differential in her favour of $1\frac{1}{2}$ knots, with an increased range without rebunkering, so that her field of possible employment was substantially broadened.

The total tramp traffic carried coastwise in vessels of over 100 gross Register tonnage in 1948 has been calculated as follows:

Cargo	Tons ('000) [30]
Coal	24 741
Cement	691
Minerals	2003
Food and feeding stuffs	1022
Miscellaneous	1027
	29 484

By 1950, many of the present-day features of the coastal shipping industry had been established. One new trade was becoming increasingly important, the trade in petroleum products and parcels of chemicals. This to some extent was to compensate for the marked diminution in coal carried coastwise as gasworks were eliminated and new kinds of fuel were planned for electricity generating stations in Britain.

The ocean trader, 1914–1950

The period immediately before the First World War was a time of prosperity for British shipping after a prolonged spell of depression, but competition was intensified as other nations equipped themselves as mercantile powers, particularly Germany, Norway and Japan. Nonetheless, Britain entered the war with nearly one-half of the world's steam tonnage, about 60 per cent of which were tramps and 40 per cent liners. This was undoubtedly the heyday of the tramp steamer, bolstered by the massive volume of coal exports and the insatiable demand for imported raw materials and foodstuffs.

The loss of British merchant shipping during the First World War aggregated 9 million gross tons,

with grievous casualties among the officers and men who served in the merchant service. Britain emerged from the war with a smaller fleet than she had in 1914, despite a vigorous war-time building programme. War-time shipbuilding was notable for the widespread adoption of standard-built ships, economizing in time of construction, labour and materials. It was a significant portent of the future that the world's first all-welded ship, *Fullagar*, was launched just after the war, in 1919.

Many shipowners confidently anticipated post-war prosperity and acquired tonnage at inflated prices, but the immediate post-war boom, accompanying the dismantling of war-time state controls,

Scottish Star, pictured here at Cape Town with a deck cargo of locomotives, was owned by Blue Star Line Ltd. A fine example of Clyde shipbuilding, she was built by Fairfield Shipbuilding and Engineering Co Ltd, a firm directly descended from the shipyard that produced the first compound-engined steamship *Brandon* in 1854. *Scottish Star*, 9996 tons gross, had a deadweight of just under 13 000 tons. Fitted with diesel engines built by Fairfield, her twin screws gave her a service speed of 16 knots. Provision was made for the accommodation of 12 first-class passengers.

was not sustained. Much of the 1920's and 1930's were troubled times for British shipowners, and tiers of laid-up ships were a dismal feature of many ports and estuaries in the depression that ensued. Recovery came only with the impending threat of war.

Of the two main shipping sectors, the liner companies best weathered the depression thanks largely to the process of amalgamation and consolidation that concentrated the ownership of liner fleets in fewer, more powerful hands that commanded great financial reserves. Most of the established firms survived, but there were some unfortunate casualties that engendered widespread distress. Critical to the survival of the liners was the consolidation of trading routes in the inter-war years as commodity patterns and flows were more fully established, but no such security was afforded to the other, the tramp, sector which depended heavily upon a buoyant trade in raw materials and coal that only world economic prosperity could sustain. Their sphere of operations was further proscribed by the advent of more specialized tonnage, especially tankers, ore carriers and refrigerated vessels in which Scandinavian and other nations played an increasing part in developing. Among other novelties in the 1920's were the construction of the first combination ore and oil freighters, as American shipbuilders designed ships to carry oil from Mexico to South America, and ore from South America to the United States. *G. Harrison Smith* (built 1921, 15 371 tons) and *Bethore* (built 1922, 8257 tons) were pioneer ship types that anticipated a notable development in such carriers in the 1950's and 1960's.

Britain's marked pre-1914 technological advantage was steadily eroded by the widespread substitution of oil fuel for coal in merchant ships, and by the more widespread adoption of diesel propulsion, in which European constructors took the lead. Britain became the victim of her long reliance upon her own resources of high quality steam coal, and many shipowners for too long pinned their hopes upon an anticipation that the pendulum would swing back in favour of coal once a revival of trade manifested itself. A few British shipowners, notably Lord Kylsant of Royal Mail Lines, Sir Frederick William Lewis of Furness, Withy, and Andrew Weir of Bank Line, embraced the potential evident in the motor ship, but perhaps with hindsight it might be thought that too many other owners showed themselves reluctant to take the plunge into what for them were uncharted waters.

The advantages of diesel propulsion were fuel economy, both in weight and space, speed and convenience in bunkering, and reduced engine-room manning. But there were corresponding drawbacks which clearly deterred many owners, notably the heavy prime cost of diesels, the high maintenance charges, and, above all, the fact that the power/weight ratio of diesel engines was for long inferior to that of steam, since there was still much scope for a marked improvement in the older mode of propulsion. Much depended upon the price and availability of coal and oil, and such uncertainties inhibited change.

Most British shipbuilders adopted Continental internal combustion engine designs, building under licence, but William Doxford & Sons of Sunderland was again among the advance guard in Britain in producing their own diesel propulsion units, first installed in the 9000 deadweight *Yngaren* in 1921 for owners in Gothenburg, Sweden.

Liner shipowners in Britain frequently selected the geared turbine as being the most cost-effective in fast cargo vessels of the highest quality, and the turbine, utilizing high pressure steam, and oil fuel in place of coal, maintained an advantage in the post-Second World War years, as exemplified by the fine 'P' class series built for Alfred Holt's Blue Funnel Line for trade to the Far East in the early 1950's.[31]

But before this, the huge toll of shipping in the Second World War had necessitated the rapid construction and commissioning of a new range of standardized ships in Britain and the United States, of which the 'Liberty' ship, evolved from the design

With many Continental tramp shipowners adopting diesel propulsion in the inter-war years, a number of British owners still pinned their faith in steam, not least those who had risen to prominence in the halcyon years of the Welsh coal trade. *South Wales* was built by Bartram & Sons Ltd of Sunderland in 1929 for the West Wales Steam Ship Co Ltd (Gibbs & Co Ltd, managers) and was a shelter-decked cargo ship of 5619 tons gross with triple-expansion engines constructed by J. Dickinson & Sons Ltd of Sunderland. In this photograph she is seen in ballast.

The Clan Line Steamers of Cayzer, Irvine & Co Ltd have had a long and distinguished history, celebrating their centenary in 1978. Their first steamer, *Clan Alpine* inaugurated a service between Glasgow, Liverpool and Bombay in 1878, and soon afterwards Calcutta, Madras, Colombo and South Africa formed part of their itinerary. By 1914, the firm had no fewer than 56 steamers, many of which were Doxford turret-deckers. The photograph depicts *Clan Mactaggart*, built by Greenock Dockyard in 1949 a 8035 gross ton cargo liner with steam turbine propulsion double-reduction geared to two screw shafts. With a service speed of 16½ knots, she carried a deadweight of 10 800 tons.

Although by no means the largest tanker of her period, Anglo-Saxon Petroleum Company *Lingula* was one of several similar products of Harland & Wolff's Belfast shipyard in the years just after the Second World War. She carried a deadweight of 9308 tons at 12 knots on a draught of 25 feet 8 inches, and was powered by oil engines designed and built in Harland & Wolff's Belfast workshops.

Gallic was originally named *War Argus*, a G Type standard merchant ship built by Workman, Clark & Co Ltd, at Belfast in 1918. Ships of her class were designed to replace wartime losses of refrigerated meat ships which had posed a threat to Britain's vital food supplies. With three decks, twin screws and triple expansion engines, *Gallic* was given a cruiser stern, then a novel feature. Owned by Oceanic Steam Navigation Co Ltd (White Star Line) of Liverpool, she was sold to Cayzer Irvine & Co in 1933 and renamed *Clan Colquhoun*, forming a unit of the Clan Line fleet until 1947 when she was sold foreign. She survived until 1956, when she was scrapped at Hong Kong.

by the Sunderland shipbuilders J.L.Thompson & Sons of *Dorington Court* (built in 1939) was the most numerous. The 'Liberty' ships, together with the various 'Empire' types, constructed in British shipyards, played a crucial rôle in maintaining the essential supplies without which Allied forces could not have survived the years of conflict.

Despite the introduction of the diesel-powered ship, the widespread adoption of oil fuel, and the greater speed and enhanced deadweight capacity of the liners and tramps of the immediate post-1944 world fleet, what would have struck the observer would have been the sense of continuity and slow evolution manifest in merchant ships of this time. Cargo handling had been greatly improved, with heavy-lift derricks fitted; loading and discharge had been further facilitated by the design of larger hatches and better hatch coverings. In the construction of ships, welding had been almost universally introduced, and the clamour of riveters was no longer the predominant sound in the world's leading shipyards.

The real revolution had not occurred by 1950, although the expert observer could perceive the portents. The super-tanker, the gas carrier, the container vessel and the roll-on-roll-off ship were soon to be evolved. The world's most remarkable shipping revolution (for that was what to follow and its history is told in the last volume of this series) was shortly to make its dramatic impact upon shipbuilders, shipowners and ports throughout the world, absorbing risk capital on an unprecedented scale. That the new capital was so effectively deployed by so many of those entrepreneurs who had sustained the evolution of the cargo ship in the 19th century exemplifies the paradox of continuity and change that characterizes that remarkable industrial sector, the shipping industry.

Standardised ships were being produced in Sunderland and other north-east coast ports in the age of wood and sail in the 1840s, and this tradition was powerfully reinforced in the steam tramp era and again in both World Wars by the urgent necessity of replacing massive war-time shipping losses. The Sunderland shipbuilding firm Joseph L. Thompson & Sons designed and built *Dorington Court* in 1939 for Court Line Ltd of London. She was a single screw steamer of economical design, having a cargo capacity of 10 200 tons and a service speed of 11 knots. This design was adopted for the first British war-time 'emergency' ship *Empire Liberty*, and formed the prototype from which the 'Liberty Ship' was evolved.

Charles M. Schwab, seen here at Southampton in August 1943 in her war-time colours, with life-rafts and guns, was built in 1943 by the Bethelehem Fairfield Shipyard Inc. for the United States War Shipping Administration. This typical 'Liberty Ship' was based upon the design that representatives of Joseph L. Thompson & Sons took to America in 1940 when there was an urgent need to replace quickly the grievous losses suffered by the Allied merchant marine in that year. In an unprecedented shipbuilding programme, more than 2700 Liberty Ships were built, one being assembled in only 4 days and 15½ hours after her keel was laid. The standard Liberty Ship registered 7176 tons gross, 4380 tons nett, and carried about 10 400 tons of dead-weight cargo at 11 knots, consuming 30 tons of coal a day.

References

1 National Maritime Museum: Lloyd's Register Survey Report: see also S.B.Martin & N.McCord, 'The steamship *Bedlington*, 1841-1854', *Maritime History* I, 1 (April 1971), pp.46-64.

2 National Maritime Museum: Lloyd's Register Survey Report.

3 C.M.Palmer, 'On the construction of iron ships and the progress of iron shipbuilding', *Industrial Resources of the Tyne, Wear and Tees* (London, 1864), p.241.

4 See J.Scott Russell, *The Modern System of Naval Architecture* II (London, 1865), Pl.64.

5 S.Seaward, 'On the practicability of shortening the duration of voyages', *Trans. Inst. Civil Engineers* III (1842), pp.385-408.

6 Geoffrey Blainey, *The Tyranny of Distance* (London, 1968), p.211.

7 John Key, 'Some personal experience . . . of marine boilers', *Trans. Hull & District Inst. of Engineers & Naval Architects* II (Sess. 1886-7), p.82.

8 See F.E.Hyde, *Blue Funnel* (Liverpool, 1957), Ch.1.

9 H.Dyer, 'On the development of the marine engine', *Proc. Glasgow Phil. Soc.* XVIII (1886-7), pp.1-27. See also *Trans. Institute of Naval Architects* (henceforth cited as *T.I.N.A.*) XXX (1889), p.102.

10 A.Blechynden, 'A review of marine engineering during the past decade', *Proc. Inst. Mechanical Engineers* (1891), pp.306ff. See also contribution to the discussion by F.C.Marshall.

11 F.C.Marshall, 'On the progress and development of the marine engine', *Proc. Inst. Mech. Eng.* (1881), pp.449ff.

12 J.McKechnie, 'Review of marine engineering during the last ten years', *Proc. Inst. Mech. Eng.* (1901), pp.607ff.

13 J.P.Hall, 'Compound and triple expansion engines', *Trans. N.E.Coast Inst. of Engineers & Shipbuilders* III (Sess. 1886-7), pp.229ff.

14 T.H.Beare, 'Abstract of results in experiments on six steamers', *Proc. Inst. Mech. Eng.* (1894), pp.33ff.

15 D.J.Lyon, *The Denny List* (Part III) (London, 1975), p.577.

16 *Lloyd's Weekly Shipping Index*, 24 Jan. 1902, p.14.

17 M.G.Mulhall, *Dictionary of Statistics* (4th ed., London, 1898), p.130.

18 B.G.Nichol & J.Gravel, 'The use and transport of liquid fuel', *Trans. N.E.Coast Inst. of Engineers & Shipbuilders* III (Sess. 1886-7), pp.27ff.

19 National Maritime Museum: (uncatalogued) C.W. Kellock papers.

20 But many 'standard' tankers built during the First World War had machinery amidships.

21 T.Westhorp in *T.I.N.A.* VIII (1867), p.19.

22 *T.I.N.A.* XLIX (1907), p.111.

23 S.J.P.Thearle, 'The evolution of the modern cargo steamer', *T.I.N.A.* XLIX (1907), p.100. Compare C.Atherton, 'On mercantile steam transport economy', *Jnl. Royal Soc. of Arts* IV (1856), p.473.

24 See Walter Runciman's evidence to *Royal Commission on Supply of Food*, Parl. Papers XXXIX (1905), Q. 10263f.

25 E.S.Meade, 'The capitalization of the International Mercantile Marine', *Political Science Quarterly* XIX, No.1 (March, 1904), p.57.

26 The comment was by W.R.Price in his evidence to *Royal Commission on Depression in Trade & Industry*, Parl. Papers XXIII (1886), Q. 10154.

27 R.Smith, *Sea-Coal for London* (London, 1961), pp.291-3.

28 D.H.Aldcroft, 'The eclipse of British coastal shipping, 1913-1921', *Journal of Transport History* VI, 1 (1963), pp.24ff.

29 L.Burnet, 'Description of a cargo-carrying coasting steamship', *Proc. Inst. Civil Engineers* LXVI (1880-1), pp.363ff.

30 P.Ford & J.A.Bound, *Coastwise Shipping & the Small Ports* (Oxford, 1951), Table III, p.16.

31 W.H.Dickie, 'High-powered single-screw cargo liners', *T.I.N.A.* XCIV (1952), pp.J1ff.

Index

Shipbuilders, Naval Architects, Inventors and Marine Engineers

Shipowners

Cargoes and Trades

THE SHIP

The first four titles in this major series of ten books on the development of the ship are: 2. *Long Ships and Round Ships: Warfare and Trade in the Mediterranean, 3000 BC–500 AD*, by John Morrison; 5. *Steam Tramps and Cargo Liners: 1850–1950*, by Robin Craig; 8. *Steam, Steel and Torpedoes: The Warship in the 19th Century*, by David Lyon; and 9. *Dreadnought to Nuclear Submarine*, by Antony Preston.

The remaining six books, which are to be published 1980–1981, will cover: 1. Ships in the ancient world outside the Mediterranean and in the medieval world in Europe (to the 15th century), by Sean McGrail; 3. The ship, from *c.*1550–*c.*1700 (including Mediterranean, Arab World, China, America); 4. The ship from *c.*1700–*c.*1820 (including Mediterranean, Arab World, China, America), both by Alan McGowan; 6. Merchant Steamships (passenger vessels), 1850–1970, by John Maber; 7. Merchant Sail of the 19th Century, by Basil Greenhill; and 10. The Revolution in Merchant Shipping, 1950–1980, by Ewan Corlett.

All titles in *The Ship* series are available from:

HER MAJESTY'S STATIONERY OFFICE
Government Bookshops

49 High Holborn, London WC1V 6HB
13a Castle Street, Edinburgh EH2 3AR
41 The Hayes, Cardiff CF1 1JW
Brazennose Street, Manchester M60 8AS
Southey House, Wine Street, Bristol BS1 2BQ
258 Broad Street, Birmingham B1 2HE
80 Chichester Street, Belfast BT1 4JY

Government publications are also available through booksellers

The full range of Museum publications is displayed and sold at
National Maritime Museum
Greenwich

Obtainable in the United States of America from Pendragon House Inc.
2595 East Bayshore Road
Palo Alto
California 94303

Cross-sections of typical bulk carrying cargo ships built between the 1870's and 1900's

Some of the constructional features of typical steamships built between 1879 and 1907 are illustrated in these cross-sections selected from J. Foster King's paper 'Structural developments in British merchant ships', printed in *Transactions of the Institute of Naval Architects*, XLIX (1907).

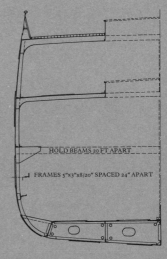

Cargo steamer 1885
LENGTH 280′ 0″   BREADTH 37′ 0″   DEPTH 26′ 0″

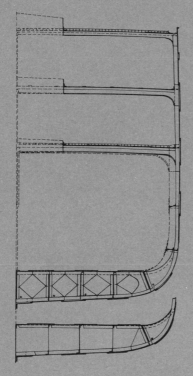

S.S. 'Buenos Ayrean' 1879
LENGTH 385′ 0″   BREADTH 42′ 0″   DEPTH 34′ 2″ & 27′ 2″

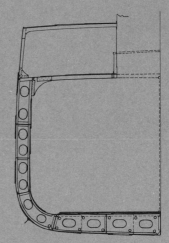

Side Tank steamer
LENGTH 325′ 0″   BREADTH 47′ 0″   DEPTH 24′ 10″